Table of Contents

List of Photographs iv

Maps vii

Chapter 1   Always in Secret
            . . . Always by Night 1

Chapter 2   Gray Wolf Holds
            Blue Python at Bay 9

Chapter 3   Sherman's Twenty-Three Days on
            "The Fringes of Hell" 23

Chapter 4   Big Blue Wave Surges
            Across Peachtree Creek 37

Chapter 5   Battle of Atlanta Lost
            After Epic Night March 51

Chapter 6   Ezra Church and Jonesboro
            Fall; Atlanta Evacuated 65

Chapter 7   Sherman Marches to Sea
            In Drive to "Ruin Georgia" 79

Index 92

List of Photographs

Gen. William Tecumseh Sherman x

Gen. Joseph Eggleston Johnston xi

The Man Who Defined War 5

Battlefield of Resaca 14

Etowah River Bridge 17

Allatoona Gap 19

Battlefield of New Hope Church 21

Federal Entrenchments 24

Soldier by Day, Priest by Night 28

Sherman's Stumbling Block 30

Crossing the Chattahoochee 40

Lt. Gen. Joseph Wheeler 42

Lt. Gen. John B. Hood 44

Brig. Gen. Braxton Bragg 45

William Key

The BATTLE of ATLANTA and the Georgia Campaign

PEACHTREE PUBLISHERS LIMITED
Atlanta, Georgia

Published by
PEACHTREE PUBLISHERS, LTD.
494 Armour Circle. N. E., Atlanta, Georgia 30324

Manufactured in the United States of America

Design by David Russell

Library of Congress Catalog No. 81-83862
ISBN: 0-931948-22-3

10 9 8 7 6 5 4 3

Col. Lemuel Grant's Fortifications 54

Potter's House 55

Brig. Gen. James B. McPherson 61

Maj. Gen. Joseph "Fighting Joe" Hooker 63

An Atlanta "Shebang" 70

The Ruins of Hood's Retreat 74

Boxcars Piled High With Household Goods 76

The End of Atlanta Depot 77

General Sherman After Capture of Atlanta 82

Atlanta Bank in Ruins 86

Union Soldiers Rip up Rails 88

✝

CHATTANOOGA

TENN.
GA.

DALTON
May 9-13

RESACA
May 14-15

CALHOUN
May 16

ADAIRSVILLE
May 17

CASSVILLE   KINGSTON
                   May 18-19

NEW HOPE CHURCH
May 25-26-27

KENNESAW MTN.   BIG SHANTY
June 10-July 2   June 8-9

ATLANTA

vii

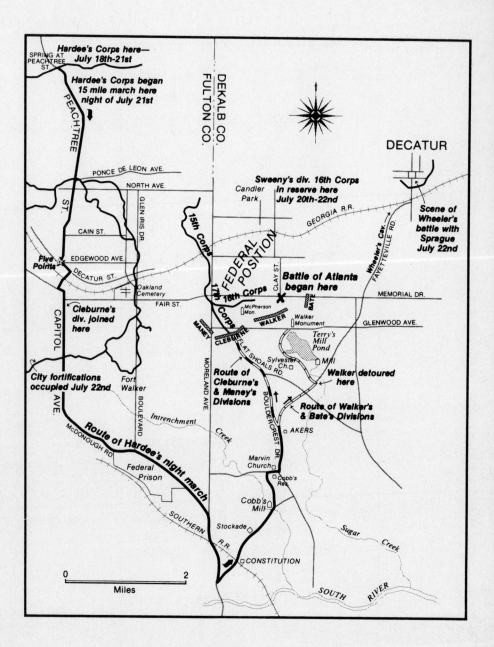

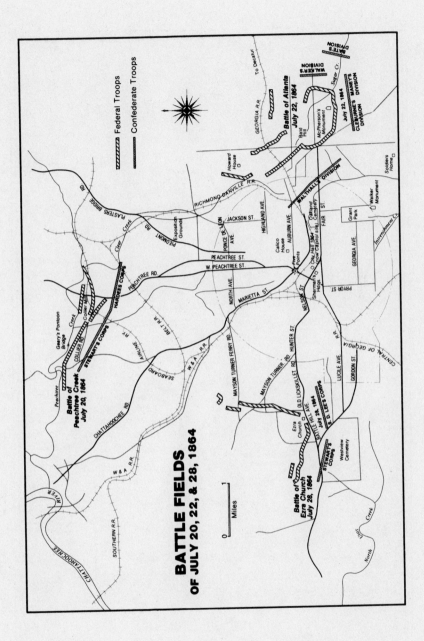

BATTLE FIELDS
OF JULY 20, 22, & 28, 1864

ix

GENERAL WILLIAM TECUMSEH SHERMAN

GENERAL JOSEPH EGGLESTON JOHNSTON

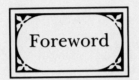

Foreword

"He knows," wrote Gene Patterson, "the song of an event as well as the size of it."

That tribute was written by Patterson, then executive editor of the *Atlanta Journal-Constitution,* a few days after the author of this book, William Obie Key, died in 1958. And in these pages, readers will understand what Patterson meant. They will hear the song, hear the shrieks and terrifying thunder of the cannonades, walk the battlefields, experience the heroics and the tragedies on both sides, and grasp the enormity of that decisive Battle of Atlanta more than a century ago.

Bill Key was a newspaperman for over three decades. He was a newspaperman's newspaperman. His colleague Ernest Rogers wrote: "His writing was clear and precise, yet flavored with that indefinable quality that made the product of his typewriter come alive on paper."

Yes, Bill Key was first and foremost a newspaperman. Yet he also was an ardent student of Civil War history, especially as the war affected his native Atlanta and Georgia. This lifelong study led him to write the precursor of this volume, a series of articles that appeared in the *Atlanta Journal-Constitution* on Sundays in 1957. Reaction from readers was phenomenal, leading to requests for, and publication of, the first edition of this book in 1958, just a few months after Bill Key's death.

Then recently the original series was again published in the

Atlanta Journal. Reaction was the same—a clamor for the book. But it was out of print and hard to find, even at libraries.

Through special arrangement with Twayne Publishers of New York, Peachtree Publishers Ltd. of Atlanta is publishing the second edition of Bill Key's original book. The only changes are where Key referred to present addresses and locations of sites of the actions and battles. Some of the old street names have since changed, some of the sites have undergone dramatic changes, especially during the building boom of the 1970s which transformed Atlanta's downtown skyline. These editing changes were made to aid the reader who may want to visit sites where specific actions took place.

Probably the finest accolade to Bill Key's book was given in a 1958 column by Harold Martin in the *Atlanta Constitution.* Martin described a visit to General George C. Marshall at Walter Reed Hospital in Washington.

"Wherever he (Bill Key) is," wrote Martin, "I hope he knows . . . that America's greatest soldier was lying there reading Bill's book and saying over and over as the beauty and the truth struck him:

"Wonderful, wonderful, wonderful."

And now, here is Bill Key's song.

Jim Rankin
Atlanta, Georgia
August, 1981

The
BATTLE
of
ATLANTA
and the
Georgia
Campaign

ALWAYS IN SECRET

. . . ALWAYS BY NIGHT

After three full desperate years of civil conflict, the beginning of the year 1864 found Union grand armies in a master invasion of Georgia soil. War had come in all its ugliness to the Empire State of the South.

True, Georgia long ago had grown accustomed—even almost callous—to the deadly struggle between North and South over the falsely advertised cause of slavery. Even such once-explosive topics as tariffs and state's rights were now only dimly mentioned—almost forgotten. It had become a deadly fight for the very existence of the South—for Georgia, for life itself.

When war first came within the boundaries of Georgia, the citizenry gave it little critical concern. The new theater was far into the northern mountainous part of the state—at least three days from Atlanta by the usual mode of travel of the day. Georgia itself was doing all right. It was maintaining twenty-one fighting regiments in the Virginia field, fighting with Robert E. Lee, and a native son, Maj. Gen. John B. Gordon, was one of Lee's most brilliant and successful commanders.

At home it had only the makeshift State Militia and the various barely trained Home Guard units of callow recruits and old men. And, of course, up where the new fighting loomed imminent, there were the Confederate armies under overall command of the brilliant Virginian, Gen. Joseph E. Johnston.

1

There, too, were Maj. Gen. William Tecumseh Sherman and his three grand armies of veteran Federal troops. But they were far away from the immediate concerns of most Georgians, viewing the gathering cloud from Atlanta on southward. At least at the time, they seemed far away.

Soon after the Union victories at Chattanooga and Lookout Mountain and the Federal defeat at Chickamauga, secret orders began to trickle down to the northern forces in Arkansas, Kentucky, Tennessee and those sections of Louisiana and Mississippi where the Federals held control.

These orders were from the Union War Department at Washington, but they merely followed out the recommendations of Lt. Gen. Ulysses S. Grant, in overall command of the United States armies, at his present headquarters at City Point, Virginia.

They were brief and to the point: every Union command post that could spare the men was to dispatch, daily if possible—but always in secret and always by night—two, three, four (though never more than five) of their most experienced soldiers. These little groups were to take along sufficient field rations and clothing and were to head for the nearest railway line that would take them southward, northward, or eastward. Their destination was kept officially secret from the selected little bands of Federal soldiers themselves. But the word soon leaked out: they were to proceed to a proper railway line where they would be picked up on signal and hauled farther east. *Destination Georgia.*

Few of the field soldiers could reason out why they were being sent to Georgia, so far from the big fight up in Virginia. Few field officers themselves understood why. But the headquarters' secret orders were obeyed. Nightly, from Union camps large and small, from all outposts where two, three, four, or sometimes five men could be trusted and spared, they went forth, knapsacks and haversacks on their backs, to make their way as best they could to the nearest rail point.

At best, it was a dark and dangerous mission. Riding the entire South, both by day and by night, were toughened veteran Confederate cavalry units, trained in the savage ways of Jeb Stuart, John Hunt Morgan and John Singleton Mosby—kill or be killed. No mile of exposed railway line in northern Mississippi and Alabama, southern Kentucky and Tennessee was safe from the swift, ghostly assaults of the Gray cavalry. No Union man traveling abroad, day or night, might regard himself as safe. But many Union soldiers—all on foot—got through, and the thin trickle from virtually every point of the compass soon began to dam up at Chattanooga, thence on down to Ringgold in Georgia to join the hordes of blue-clad forces under the overall command of a restless and fuming Sherman.

Many of the brave and adventurous Northern soldiers never completed their mission. Some were caught in the open and taken prisoner and sent on down to Georgia to the vile prison camp at Andersonville. Some were challenged and elected to fight it out. They died in their tracks. Some tried subterfuge.

There were the Mayfield brothers, from Indiana, John, Elbert and Willie Mayfield, ages 19, 17 and 16, respectively. Proud of their newly issued winter uniforms, these young farm brothers devised a fatal way to keep them fresh and unsoiled during their long secret trek from northern Louisiana to an undetermined railhead to the north. They removed their uniforms, carefully rolled them up, obtained and attired themselves in slovenly farmhand's overalls, coats and clog shoes. The eldest, John, expressed some misgivings. "They might hang us, in these clothes," he pointed out. The youngest, Willie, scoffed: "They got to catch us first." They mulled it over. "Shucks," said Elbert, "they wouldn't hang us, would they—just for keeping our uniforms neat?" "No, I guess not," John decided. But they did. They were caught, and their explanation seemed too weak to the now-hardened Southern guerrillas, who a couple of years before might have merely taken them prisoner. Their young bodies, in ragged farmhand clothes, with the new uniforms neatly strapped under their arms, swung crazily from moss-festooned trees the morning after they were stopped.

While the rank and file of the Northern soldiery could see little advantage to be gained in a conquest of Georgia, the necessity was crystal-clear to the Union military genius.

Lee, in Virginia, was infuriating the Northern high command by his series of brilliant offensive and defensive movements. He could do this only so long as he could depend upon Georgia to keep vital supplies coming by rail up through the Carolinas to his depots. There had been bloody draft revolts in Northern cities, bloodier slaughter of helpless blacks caught in the maelstrom of a war ostensibly over their freedom but which cruelly ignored them in all practical and human ways. Hundreds of poor, defenseless blacks had been slaughtered, burned to death and hanged from lampposts in New York City for a reason no more logical than that they were black and therefore the cause of the war that was bleeding white a weary North.

Grant, in overall command at City Point, Virginia, thought he could stop Lee if only some means were found to bring a halt to the river of supplies that rolled up on every train from Georgia. (Latter-day military experts held that, even without the manpower of the Georgia theater, a properly provisioned Lee, with twenty thousand men, could have roamed at will up and down the Shenandoah Valley for twenty years. But the provisions were a daily necessity; therefore Georgia, with its bursting warehouses of meat and grain, its manufactories of shoes, clothing, vehicles, munitions and weapons, was his right arm. In fact, by 1864, Georgia had become the very heartbeat of the Confederacy, while Virginia was important chiefly as a possible gateway to Northern invasion.)

Sherman for nearly a century has been damned as a brutal, conscienceless commander. To the extent that he did not allow chivalric attitudes deter him, this was true. It may even be true that Sherman had a callous streak as a military man. Some of his official statements betray a viciousness rarely seen in most high military men. It was equally true that he nurtured an almost personal vindictiveness against the populace of Georgia rather than against its purely military objectives. His wholesale deportation of the entire population of the little town of Roswell, Georgia, to hostile and alien Indiana during the height of a civil war, may attest to this streak. But Sherman was an able commander. He knew that of all the states then fighting the Union, Georgia loomed as the chief and staunchest provider.

Every captured wagon in virtually all of the campaigns in which Sherman had held command had borne the tantalizing label "Made in Atlanta." Just about every other of the chief sinews of war also boasted the hated brand "Made in Atlanta," including splendid

4

THE MAN WHO DEFINED WAR—William Tecumseh Sherman (leaning on cannon's breech) and his staff.
(Library of Congress photo)

revolvers, scabbards and swords, shoes and uniforms. But the principal reason Sherman decided—and it was he who persuaded Grant that Georgia must be overpowered if the war was to be won by the North—on the Georgia Campaign was the fact that Atlanta, one of the state's five largest cities, lay at the center of a crossroads of iron by virtue of the four railways that entered the growing little city.

By the close of 1863 the value of the railroads as an important adjunct to fighting and winning a war had been proved. It was true that the new means of transportation had been utilized to some extent as early as 1846, when a regiment of Pennsylvania volunteers moved to New Orleans to join General Scott's army in its drive to capture Mexico City. In that same year, 1846, the Prussian army had moved an entire division of twelve thousand men by rail. During the Crimean War, the British built a railroad only seven miles long to aid in supplying troops and evacuating the wounded during the siege of Sevastopol (1854-55).

However, it was not until the American Civil War that there occurred the first real "railroad war." In 1861, Confederate troops gave the slip to the Federals who were watching their movements in Virginia and were rushed by railway trains of the Manassas Gap Railroad across the Blue Ridge Mountains. The troops, forming up as they left the cars within sound of the battle guns, reached the battlefield of First Bull Run (Manassas) in time to outflank the Union forces and put the North in complete rout.

Confederate armies had been moved by rail from Tupelo, Mississippi, to Chattanooga, Tennessee, in eight days, a distance of only two hundred and seventy-five miles by direct route. But the strategy of this feat lay in the fact that the rail movement did not run directly from Tupelo to Chattanooga. Instead, because of the available rail lines, the Confederate army had to be moved a total of nine hundred miles from Tupelo down to Mobile, Alabama, across a twenty-mile stretch of water by ferry, thence on up northward to Chattanooga. And perhaps the most dramatic movement of armed forces in history to that date was when, in September, 1863, during a lull following the bloody Battle of Gettysburg, three divisions of General "Dutch" Longstreet's corps were sent from Lee's command in Virginia to reinforce Maj. Gen. Braxton Bragg, facing Federal

Maj. Gen. William S. Rosecrans in a struggle for the important rail junction at Chattanooga.

This latter move involved five brigades of Confederate infantry, with supporting artillery, for a distance of eight hundred and thirty-five miles, via Weldon, North Carolina, to Augusta and on to Atlanta, over single track of varying gauges, thence on to Chickamauga. Maj. Gen. John B. Hood (later to relieve Johnston of command during the seige of Atlanta) is reported to have jumped his horse from the railway car door, riding to the boom of cannon along the banks of the Chickamauga, so-called "River of Death."

It was Sherman who reached the decision that Atlanta and all of Georgia must be subjected because of its strategic center of Confederate supply, largely due to the state's railroads converging on the city.

Thus, Sherman, whose military adroitness had never been in question, decided that Georgia must be crushed. Grant, in far Virginia, saw the merit behind the recommendation, but Grant never acquiesced in some of the more ruthless proposals submitted by his able chief Southern fighter. Privately, Grant knew that the younger general in command in the Deep South was a wholehearted worshipper of Grant's methods of warfare. He also knew that it was said Sherman actually tried to imitate the Federal commander in chief both in tactics and in personal demeanor. Some of Sherman's critics attributed this inclination to ape Grant to Sherman's dislike of "dressing up" or shaving too regularly. Grant secretly may have been pleased at his junior chief officer, but he never gave Sherman *carte blanche* in his every request to proceed with harsh vigor. In this respect, Grant deserves history's accolade as being the more humane of the two generals.

7

GRAY WOLF HOLDS
BLUE PYTHON AT BAY

Atlanta's population officially was listed in the 1860 census at 9,554 inhabitants. But by the beginning of 1864, to this official number had been added thousands more who had sought refuge from both north and south Georgia. The actual population was nearer eighteen thousand.

The center of Atlanta then, as now, was called Five Points, and in 1864 the town's outermost limits extended in all directions not much more than fifteen present city blocks.

Small as it was, the little city of Atlanta was being watched in Richmond, in Washington, in various cities of the North and West, and in Europe too.

Atlanta had become the unofficial capital of the Confederacy. Richmond and Virginia constituted the only other main sector of the terrible War Between the States (as the South insisted on calling it)—a war that had been dragging on for three years. Virginia was the northern gateway, and it was important chiefly because it offered an avenue of still possible invasion of the great northern cities—Washington, Philadelphia, New York, even Boston.

But Georgia was as vital as Virginia, if not more so, as the single great breadbasket for the South's two remaining grand armies, now in Georgia and Virginia. The former was under the overall command of Gen. Joseph E. Johnston, and the latter under the incomparable Robert E. Lee.

Lee and Johnston were both superb fighting men. Grant ranked the small-statured Johnston ahead of Lee. "I was always anxious," he said publicly, "with Johnston at my front. I was never so concerned when I faced Lee."

Joe Johnston was a strange general. Seldom lucky in an advance, he has been described as dangerous as a running wolf in retreat. Sherman said of him that his retreats were always matchless military maneuvers. Johnston seldom left anything behind but a badly chastised foe, keeping his own forces almost intact. He had a deep personal regard for human lives—a remarkable trait for a soldier.

The anxieties of the North were understood even by the southern layman in May, 1864. If either Lee in Virginia or Johnston in Georgia were victorious, one or the other could fight his way southward or northward, join forces with the other, and form the most dangerous combined armed threat the North had yet faced.

But Lee, who was on a winning streak in Virginia, had to depend almost solely on Georgia for his food, clothing and supplies, and, in a pinch, could depend on fighting reinforcements from Georgia.

The reason was simple: Georgia furnished the food and Atlanta's thriving factories made the munitions, guns, saddles, clothing and other basic supplies. And, above all else, Atlanta stood at the center of a cross of railroads. Four main lines diverged from the city in 1864: the Western & Atlantic, to Chattanooga; the Georgia Railroad, to Augusta, connecting with Charleston, Wilmington, and on up to Norfolk and other Virginia points; the Macon and Western, to Macon and on to Savannah; and the Atlanta & West Point, to points in Alabama, Mobile among them.

The first week of May, 1864, did not find Atlanta very much excited about the opening of the Georgia Campaign to the north. To the Atlantan of that year, Dalton was a very faraway place, and Johnston, next to Lee, in Atlanta's mind, was the South's greatest fighter. He would never allow Sherman to get within cannonshot of the city. In those days a person traveled by horse or horse and buggy no more than twenty or thirty miles in a day. So Atlanta, a little hungry, a great deal threadbare, went about its daily customs, mourning its dead in secret, smiling bravely in public. That first week of May, 1864, saw eight grand balls held in Atlanta, notwithstanding that every hospital, every hotel and boarding-house, and most of the large private homes were filled with wounded Confederate soldiers. The ladies of Altanta helped care for the wounded, attended dances at night, joined the Home Guard boys in singing the sweet, sad words of the popular song "Lorena," or smiled at the wounded boys whooping it up with "Jine the Cavalry." On Sundays the people drove or walked out to "those crazy forts"—a ten-mile irregular circle of deep trenches, breast-works, redoubts, platforms and rifle pits the slaves had been paid a dollar a day for putting up around the city for the last year. (The slaves didn't receive the dollar a day; it was paid to their owners.) But, worried? No; Atlanta wasn't at all concerned over the fantastic nightmare of being invaded by the rough-bearded Sherman.

In Europe the watchers daily kept up with news from Georgia. Avidly they read every word concerning the disposition of each of the grand armies: Sherman was at Ringgold, some twenty miles north of Dalton, where Johnston recently had been placed in supreme command after Braxton Bragg's defeats.

The watchers in Europe kept posted. Chief among them, sniffing the air for the long-dreamed-of chance of defying the hated Monroe Doctrine, was Louis Napoleon, emperor of France, ready to jump in and tip the scales in favor of the Confederacy if the fortunes of war favored Johnston's and Lee's armies.

In Spain the intriguing ministers of the inept Isabella II watched with keen anticipation when the wind blew against the United States.

In England Lord John Palmerston, the prime minister, had long favored the South. His foreign minister, Lord John Russell, had sided with the North after Raphael Semmes had taken the valorous English-built raider, the *Alabama,* out on the dark and dangerous Atlantic to sink, thus far, sixty-five United States ships. These two watched, each hopeful of a victory for his choice.

At this particular time sentiment in the northern United States was such that any definite large-scale defeat of the Union armies would have brought about a negotiated peace. The general public was clamoring for such an end to the bloodletting. One or two major defeats would have turned the trick, and the military leaders on both sides realized this.

Such was the situation—the temperament, the outsiders' views and attitudes, the physical anatomy of the Georgia and Virginia battle scenes—when Sherman, at Ringgold, decided on May 7 to launch an all-out assault on all of Georgia to the southward of Johnston's forces at Dalton. He had the determination; he had the incentive.

And he knew he had the men, the officers, the will.

Let us examine these grand armies facing each other in north Georgia that first week in May, 1864.

The makeup of those armies lists names that were to live in history and to be revered in heroic granite and bronze more than a century after the Atlanta campaign was over.

On the Union side, in overall command during the entire Georgia Campaign, was Maj. Gen. William Tecumseh Sherman, heading three large Federal armies as follows:

The Army of the Cumberland consisted of four full corps—the Fourth, the Fourteenth, the Twentieth and a cavalry corps. Each corps consisted of three full divisions, under overall corps command of Maj. Gen. George H. Thomas.

The Army of the Tennessee consisted of three full corps—the Fifteenth, Sixteenth and Seventeenth. The Fifteenth made up four divisions, and the other two, two divisions each. These were under the overall corps command of Maj. Gen. James B. McPherson until July 22, when McPherson was killed in the Battle of Atlanta. From July 22 until July 27, it was commanded by Maj. Gen. John A. Logan; then it was taken over by Maj. Gen. Oliver O. Howard.

The Army of the Ohio consisted of one full corps, the Twenty-third, made up of three divisions under command of Maj. Gen. John M. Schofield; and one cavalry division under Maj. Gen. George Stoneman.

Sherman's full strength on May 1, 1864, officially was listed as 110,123 men. With reinforcements as the campaign got under way, this strength went up to 112,819 on June 1. However by July 1, it was listed at 106,070, showing the beginning of the heavy casualties exacted in the north Georgia fighting. By August 1, Sherman's

106,070 men had been slashed to 91,675, and by September 1, to 81,758 men.

On the Confederate side, in overall command was General Johnston. The Confederate army did not list its corps by the numbered system but rather by the names of their ranking commanders. It is also interesting to note another peculiarity in the designation of Southern fighting units as compared to those of the Union forces: while the Northern grand armies were usually named for rivers—Army of the Potomac, Army of the Ohio, Army of the Cumberland, and the like—the Confederate main armies were always named for states or localities—Army of Northern Virginia, Army of Mississippi, and so on. The armies in Georgia under Johnston officially were registered on the lists as the "Army of Tennessee." But since the Union Army of the Tennessee was prominently engaged in the Georgia campaign, it would puzzle the reader to refer to the Southern army as the "Army of Tennessee." Most historians therefore, have dropped that appellation in describing its activities.

In overall command of the Confederate army, as has been said, was General Johnston. Under Johnston were the following corps:

Hardee's Corps of four divisions, under Lt. Gen. William J. Hardee;

Hood's Corps of three divisions, under command of Lt. Gen. John B. Hood;

Wheeler's Cavalry Corps of three divisions, under Lt. Gen. Joseph Wheeler;

Polk's Corps of three divisions, under Lt. Gen. Leonidas Polk;

One artillery division of four battalions, under Brig. Gen. F. A. Shoup; and

One cavalry brigade under Brig. Gen. W. H. Jackson.

Johnston's full official strength on May 1, 1864, was listed as 42,856 men.

Sherman's artillery consisted of two hundred and fifty-four cannon or other big guns; Johnston's, one hundred and twenty cannon.

In Atlanta, as the Georgia Campaign opened to the north, there was no scarcity of news. At one time in the growing little city there

13

BATTLEFIELD OF RESACA — Scene of the first heavy fighting. (Library of Congress photo)

were as many as seven daily newspapers publishing at once. During the latter part of 1863, publishers from Memphis, Knoxville, and Chattanooga, with some parts of their editorial staffs, moved to Atlanta. The city itself during that period had supported four dailies: the *Intelligencer*, the *Southern Confederacy*, the *Reveille*, and the *Commonwealth*. Refugee editors from Tennessee set up in Atlanta the *Chattanooga Rebel*, the *Knoxville Register,* and the *Memphis Appeal.* All these papers were issued daily—or almost daily—and they were printed on a wide variety of paper, ranging from fine bookpaper, pure white commercial paper, through straw-colored rough stock, manila, common brown wrapping paper—even wallpaper. When the *Chattanooga Rebel* had to run out of Atlanta ahead of Sherman, it printed successively as a daily in Griffin, Macon and Columbus, in Georgia; and in Selma, Alabama. One of its editorial associates in all these jaunts was Henry Watterson, later to become world-famous as "Marse Henry" Watterson of the equally famous *Louisville Courier-Journal* in Kentucky.

The winter of 1863-64 had been a cruel one in north Georgia. Snow, sleet and freezing rains had given way to high, cold winds and long periods of dark, leaden skies. But the first week of May, 1864, brought a promise of genuine spring, and on May 8 Sherman issued general orders for the advance southward into Georgia.

Johnston at Dalton, with the impregnable heights of Rocky Face between him and Sherman, decided not to try a major stand against the mighty Blue mass advancing from Ringgold. He received word that Sherman had ordered McPherson's tough Army of the Tennessee to start a flanking movement around the Confederates' position at Dalton. He also knew that the entire Federal armies, with the exception of the Fourth Corps of General Thomas' Army of the Cumberland, would follow McPherson within a few days.

McPherson's thick Blue columns swung for the narrow defiles of Snake Creek Gap, their immediate destination being Resaca, eighteen miles south.

It was at this point in the Atlanta Campaign that the superb but simple thinking of "Old Joe" Johnston outwitted the hard-bitten field marshalship of Sherman.

15

Knowing that Sherman's two other big armies would follow at McPherson's heels through the tight pass at Snake Creek, Johnston resorted to seventh-grade arithmetic to set his course of action. It would, he reckoned, take more than twice as much time for one hundred and ten thousand men to sneak through a narrow pass and reach Resaca, eighteen miles to his south, than it would for an army of forty-two thousand to go almost by direct roadway to Resaca, where he already had set up strong rearguard positions.

Therefore, holding onto Dalton until the last minute, Johnston waited until the Federals jammed Snake Creek Pass in a giant bottleneck before he moved his main army out of Dalton, on the night of May 12, reaching Resaca the morning of the next day ahead of the main Union forces.

Meanwhile, Johnston's strong rearguard at Resaca twice had hurled back the probings of McPherson's Army of the Tennessee while Johnston arrived in force and took his position. Sherman immediately tried to pry him out, launching a mass attack, but failed to dislodge the Gray lines at Resaca. Instead, Sherman's big Blue python drew back with considerable damage.

At the same time Sherman recoiled, however, he decided on another flanking strategy, sending McPherson's army around Johnston by crossing the Oostanaula River.

McPherson's crossing was made at a place called Lay's Ferry just south of Resaca. Once again Johnston, hearing of the move, found his rear and lines of communication threatened, especially along the Western & Atlantic Railroad.

This railroad more than ever had become the desperate prize of both Sherman and Johnston. Sherman used it for men and supplies from as far away as Nashville, Tennessee, as he advanced into Georgia. Johnston all the while had to depend upon the railroad for his own supplies, for a trickle of reinforcements, and as a means of sending wounded men to Atlanta.

So once more "Old Joe," as his men affectionately called him, became the running Gray Wolf, slashing fiercely at the encircling Blue python as he began yet another withdrawal. At this point, Johnston found himself more than usually hard-pressed by McPherson's rearward thrust and Sherman's continued onslaughts from the north. The Confederate general was seeking desperately

ETOWAH RIVER BRIDGE – Johnston crossed here on his way to Allatoona.
(National Archives photo)

for a defensive position of strength around Adairsville. And he couldn't find a single spot where he could dig in and make a stand.

Therefore he had no alternative but to retreat farther—this time to Cassville, near Cartersville. It was here that Johnston seems to have undergone a rare change of temperament. He announced to his general staff that he would stand and make a full fight at Cassville. But his corps commanders didn't like the idea at all. All but Hardee, whose corps was the weakest of the entire army, disagreed strongly; and Johnston changed his mind, against his will. Once more the little Gray army was on the retreat, whittling in daily skirmishes at the advancing Blue columns, delaying its advance. The soldiers were tired—dog-tired.

On May 20, with a hot sun high overhead, Johnston took his army of veteran fighters across the Etowah River into the rough hill country near Allatoona Pass. There was a trick up his gray sleeve, which, if Sherman fell for the bait, might give the South a major victory.

And Sherman came within an inch of falling for Johnston's strategy. Indeed, Sherman had just about made up his mind to pursue hotly his wily adversary into the hilly wilds around Allatoona Pass, when a phenomenal flash of memory saved the Federal chief.

Twenty years before, in 1844, Sherman as a young first lieutenant had served a tour of duty in Georgia, being stationed at Marietta. He had ridden far and wide over the north Georgia terrain, especially in the vicinity of Allatoona Gap. The Union officer had a singular whimsy which he described to close friends as a "pure love for land—just land itself." He incidentally possessed the unique ability to recall, visually, the topography of any land he had ever viewed. Now he realized that any mass frontal attack on the Gray Wolf in that rocky, hilly land around Allatoona would be suicidal. He changed his mind just before he was about to give the order for the mass assault.

Instead, Sherman snaked his long Blue columns through the loblolly pines and scrub oak and gullies, around the trenches of the Gray Wolf, around Kingston and on down to the more protective terrain of Paulding County.

But the Gray Wolf was not to be caught by Sherman's familiar flanking strategy, which this time had taken the Federal chief too far

ALLATOONA GAP — Just to the right of the middle of this photo, as viewed from the bridge. Johnston's rear guard fortifications are in the foreground. (Library of Congress photo)

away from the vital W & A Railroad lines. By parallel road from Allatoona, Johnston quick-marched his small army southward to a section that was to enthrall the pages of future histories under the identity of New Hope Church. This spot lay about five miles north of Dallas, from which little community a number of roads fingered the way toward Atlanta.

Johnston got there first with fewer men, but he grimly blocked those divergent roadways, and once again the shadow of the Gray saber parried the threat of the Blue bayonet pointed at Atlanta.

It had rained the night of May 24, but the next day broke fair and hot. By minutes it grew hotter, the distant landscape shimmering in visible waves of heat. May steamed from the earth, rich and sweet. A perfumed lavender haze hung shoulder-high above the freshened land as the curtain rose on one of the deadliest engagements of the Georgia Campaign.

Sherman paced his headquarters area muttering to himself. This was a characteristic which, when he first came to the supreme command, caused his soldiers to refer to him as "that crazy new general." Now he was in the throes of fateful decision—to attack or not to attack. Abruptly he reached the decision to attack Johnston on his front—a decision he years later admitted he almost instantly regretted.

The Federals opened up with a smashing assault—with everything they had—against Johnston's entrenched Gray defenders. To the South it would always be the Battle of New Hope Church. But the soldiers in blue remembered it to their dying day as the Battle of the Hell Hole. Union losses at the end of four days' hard fighting—four days which saw ceaseless cannon and rifle fire, charge and countercharge, and naked bayonet against clubbed musket—totaled upwards of three thousand men. Johnston's casualties were nine hundred.

Now it came home to Sherman with alarming clarity that he had led his soldiers too far away from the railroad tracks. His position daily was becoming more awkward, his supplies running dangerously low. So after a series of skirmishes in force, he fought his way, on June 7, back to the railroad at Acworth. But he didn't stop there. He moved on down to a place then called Big Shanty, now

BATTLEFIELD OF NEW HOPE CHURCH — One of the deadliest battles of the Georgia Campaign. Northern casualties, three thousand; Confederates, nine hundred. (Library of Congress photo)

Kennesaw. He then felt safer, back on the railroad and at a place where he could dig in and get his breath.

Before he could fairly draw an easy breath, however, his scouts brought him word that set the rough-bearded warrior to talking to himself again: Johnston, in force, had slipped around the entire Blue lines and had entrenched himself solidly around the base and well up the slopes of Kennesaw Mountain and had manned to some extent two nearby mountains called Pine Mountain and Lost Mountain. Not only that, Johnston had succeeded in dragging all of his heavy cannon far up the sides of Kennesaw. And these three eminences, particularly Kennesaw, controlled Sherman's direct route to Atlanta, twenty-two miles away.

Flabbergasted, Sherman decided that here and now was as good a place and time as any for a showdown battle. His decision was to result in a full twenty-three days of the bloodiest and most hopeless task the brusque Sherman had undertaken up to this time in any campaign of the entire Civil War.

SHERMAN'S TWENTY-THREE DAYS

ON "THE FRINGES OF HELL"

One of the oddest puzzles of the entire Atlanta Campaign is why the veteran and clever Sherman decided to make a general all-out assault on Joe Johnston's forces on Kennesaw Mountain.

The Confederate general in chief had shown his remarkable genius in retreat. He also had forced Sherman to retreat in the frightful battle of New Hope Church. Johnston's army was known by Sherman to be the very cream of the South's fighting men—all bone-tough, hardened veterans who would follow "Old Joe," their personal hero, anywhere there was fighting to be done.

Why did Sherman, who had declined a major engagement with the Confederates at Allatoona Pass because he felt the wild, hilly terrain would make such an assault suicidal, now make the decision to attempt a vastly more dangerous and difficult movement by going up the steep sides of Kennesaw when Allatoona's lesser defenses had scared him off?

There are many suggested reasons why the northern commander in chief reached his desperate decision to attack Kennesaw Mountain—a decision which was to bring about the bloodiest encounter Sherman thus far had engaged in in the entire war. It was a decision that was to end in costly failure, so far as its immediate objectives were concerned.

One reason Sherman felt Johnston's army had to be driven from Kennesaw Mountain, as explained by a Federal general years

FEDERAL ENTRENCHMENTS—At the foot of Kennesaw Mountain. (Library of Congress photo)

later, was that Johnston's high position "made an impregnable military position . . . overlooking the country in all directions which made concealment of movements on Sherman's part next to impossible."

Another reason, no doubt, was that Sherman's long line of supply was daily growing longer. It now ran, so far as supplies themselves were concerned, from Chattanooga, more than a hundred miles north. For reinforcement of men, it ran all the way back to Nashville, and Sherman reported that it was necessary, day and night, to "guard every foot of the railroad" against sneak attacks by guerrilla bands of Confederates. If he lost the W & A Railroad at this point in the grim war game, his armies were as good as beaten.

There also was a very natural reason—the temptation of a quick, decisive defeat of the Confederate armies in Georgia. If Sherman could split those forces by a heavy assault, even if costly, on Kennesaw's slopes, it was, to Sherman, worth the try.

But there was still another influential reason. Abraham Lincoln in June, 1864, stood on the very threshhold of political defeat. The northern states were growing daily weary of the war with the repeated news of defeats in Virginia, the call for more men, and the drain on the economy. Public officials, newspaper editors and the people at large were openly talking about bringing an end to the terrible conflict through a negotiated peace.

One big victory, one surprising, colorful major blow would give the North a shot in the arm, would reelect Lincoln, and would no doubt win the war.

Twenty-two miles approximately south of Kennesaw Mountain, the people of Atlanta were beginning to worry a little. There was a lot of talk in the streets, and wherever folks met, the first thing they said was, "Why does Johnston keep on retreating? Why doesn't he stand and make a fight?" Others, more pessimistic, grumbled, "Give us a general who'll fight." The better informed citizenry knew that Joe Johnston on Kennesaw Mountain, even though outnumbered nearly three to one, was in a better military position than he had been in since the retreat began at Dalton. Meanwhile, prices of food in Atlanta were so high that most of the people were concocting odds-and-ends dishes which were humorously called "Confederate fricassee," "blockade pudding,"and "Sherman hash." Willow-bark tea was becoming popular as a beverage. "Hey, what's Sherman hash made out of?" a friend, meeting another, would ask. "Dunno. Tastes kinda like hit's made outta Ole Sherman's britches," was the standard reply. And the usual rejoinder, "Wal, hit won't taste like that long. Ole Joe's gonna git a-holt of them britches pretty soon now." Some quotable prices: flour $2.50 a pound, poor quality; sugar $15 to $20 a pound; butter $12; beef (surprisingly low) $6 to $7.50 a pound; coffee $25 a pound; sweet potatoes $25 a bushel; syrup $30 a gallon ("sweetenin' is gittin' mighty sca'ce"). Some Atlantans of 1864 plunked down the high prices; others did without. All began to tighten their belts a little snugger.

On June 10, 1864, Sherman gave the fateful order. The die was cast; more than one hundred and fifty thousand men were poised for what would become one of the most fearful battles in the annals of warfare up to that time. It lasted twenty-three days, and the slopes of Kennesaw Mountain were literally drenched with blood in an epic struggle that would leave the shaggy green tower a natural monument to American heroes who fought to the death. Each side fought for a different cause, and each side was convinced its cause was right.

Sherman's three grand armies maneuvered into position, moving up from the railroad station at Kennesaw to the ground within a quarter of a mile of the base of Kennesaw Mountain. During the next three or four days, the cavalry of both sides engaged in ferocious clashes. The Federal cavalry was led by General Stoneman, while Gen. Joseph Wheeler was in the saddle for the Grays.

In this cavalry skirmishing, the W & A Railroad tracks were without any doubt the objective—that frail iron lifeline to the north for Sherman, the thin metal vein that kept Joe Johnston's feeble flow of supplies and, on occasion, reinforcements from the south, trickling up to Marietta. The Gray cavalry cut the bridge across the Etowah to the north, the Blue engineers on June 12 repaired it again, and on the steep sides of Kennesaw the men in the revetted trenches heard the far wail of the first locomotive in days bringing Sherman more men and supplies from the north.

Closer, ever closer to the dangerous base of Kennesaw Mountain Sherman edged his three armies. Something soon must give. The Confederates' line was thinly extended to the heights of Pine and Lost Mountains, which, with Kennesaw, stood as three sentinels in Sherman's straight path to Atlanta.

The Confederates, looking over their ten-mile line, suddenly decided to pull in—all to Kennesaw's twin heights. The decision was a smart move on Johnston's part, but it brought tragedy that was felt throughout the South.

On June 14, at about 2 o'clock in the afternoon, Generals Johnston, Hardee, and Polk went up on Pine Mountain to look over the land. They sat upon their horses far up the side of Pine and reached the decision to pull in their forces to Kennesaw. Gen. Leonidas Polk gave one look over the land below. Strange indeed was this man—a tough, fierce soldier and an ordained priest. The ranking Episcopal bishop of Louisiana, Polk had donned priestly robes on May 11 at Dalton to baptize his friend, Gen. John B. Hood, who on that night in church assembly had publicly announced his desires to "join the Army of the Lord." Bishop-General Polk performed the ritual.

A quarter of a mile away, on a lesser hill, General Sherman squinted through his glasses across the valley and saw a throng of mounted and unmounted gray figures near the top of Pine Mountain. It irritated the Union chieftain, who turned to a colonel of artillery and snapped, "Have one of your guns throw a shell over there and break up that congregation!"

A sweating Union cannoneer, stripped to the waist in the hot sun, yanked the lanyard on a twelve-pound Parrott gun. The roar reverberated through the hot hills. Over on Pine Mountain, Generals Johnston, Polk and Hardee reined their mounts to go down the mountain. A cannonball ripped the Episcopal bishop-general from left to right through the chest. He was dead before he toppled from his rearing horse. (The next day, in Atlanta, the biggest funeral of the war was held for Polk in St. Luke's Episcopal Church, which stood on the present corner of Broad and Walton streets, where now stands the Broad Street entrance to the Grant Building.)

SOLDIER BY DAY, PRIEST BY NIGHT—Lt. Gen. Leonidas Polk. He was Episcopal bishop of Louisiana and was killed by a cannon-ball on Pine Mountain. (Library of Congress photo)

On the day of Polk's funeral in Atlanta, a half-crazy slave, walking along Washington Street, stopped and mounted the top of a large gatepost. He had got hold of some forbidden liquor, and the odd quiet of the city, together with the liquor and the funeral holiday he was enjoying from digging trenches, set him off on a queer tangent. Atop the gatepost he began to preach a sermon in an almost-forgotten Bantu dialect, mixing it with a hazy remembrance of Biblical quotations. The lady of the house came to the porch in annoyance and saw what was going on. She went inside, got a broom, and made threatening gestures at the slave. When her dog came out, the slave hopped from his perch and skedaddled down the street, half a dozen neighborhood dogs in yapping pursuit.

"Skedaddle." That was a new Yankee word Atlanta was coming to use and like. It sounded comical, rolled easily around the tongue, and was expressive of somebody getting away in a hurry. The city had another Yankee word it took to—"shebang." A shebang was almost any place you could dig out to make enough room to crawl in, put a jute or tarpaper cover on, and keep out the elements. Soon Atlantans were going to dig many shebangs—along the railroad tracks, in sides of hills, or anywhere to keep out shell fragments and red-hot cannonballs.

Sherman sent his first massive thrust against the Confederates on Kennesaw on June 15. Three divisions of McPherson's army advanced and succeeded in capturing a spur in the foothills which overlooked Hood's entrenched first line of skirmishers. Hood thus was forced back behind a creek called Noonday. It was a bad start for the southerners, for an entire Alabama regiment was taken prisoner by the Federals.

At about the same time, Thomas's Army of the Cumberland, a field force in excess of fifty thousand men, also rammed forward. But the Gray line held for several hours in the face of Thomas's thrust, together with Maj. Gen. "Fighting Joe" Hooker's entire corps. But Hooker persisted, was victorious, and captured the Confederate trench in this sector.

Then "Fighting Joe" hurled an entire division at the Confederate main line. But here he ran head-on into Confederate Maj. Gen. Pat Cleburne. It was a byword in Cleburne's outfit that "Nobody

29

SHERMAN'S STUMBLING BLOCK—Kennesaw Mountain, seen on the distant horizon. Here, Johnston took his stand. (National Archives photo)

ever takes anything away from Pat Cleburne." They didn't that day, either. The peppery Confederate general drove the Union attackers back with terrific losses, including several hundred prisoners.

Rain had been falling daily for more than two weeks. The trenches and rifle pits on both sides were quagmires, and the wet slopes of Kennesaw were as slippery as glass. Both forces frequently battled it out amid thunderstorms in which they could not distinguish between the roar of cannon and the rolling thunderclaps. At night the entire mountain was lighted up with little blue-white muzzle flashes from musketry and the big reddish blobs of cannon fire.

Kennesaw Mountain has twin crests, one slightly higher than the other, with a "saddle" connecting the two peaks. Johnston placed big gun batteries on both crests, and on the morning of June 22, a furious double bombardment opened upon the Federals below and downslope in the valley. The solid shot, high explosive shells, and grapeshot struck with deadly accuracy the Union camps and trenches below, including the units and wagon trains in the open fields. By noon a general and disorderly retreat of Union forces was under way. It continued all day and all night.

Sherman was angered by this bombardment. He drew his main forces out of range and ordered 140 big guns brought up and concentrated on the Confederate battery positions atop Kennesaw's twin peaks. For two whole days the Federal battery poured a ceaseless fire on the Gray artillery positions. Twenty-two miles southward in Atlanta, the booming guns of Kennesaw sounded like a dread overture of doom—a prelude to disaster.

An unmailed letter from a dead young Union captain to his father in Pennsylvania read:

"For two weeks now we have been camped on the very fringes of Hell, a mountain called on the maps Kennesaw. Our general seems determined to take the mountain, but the Rebels seem just as determined we shan't. I will be glad when this one is behind us. . ."

Sherman's three-to-one forces were probing everywhere in the long Gray defense line for a weak spot, but Johnston managed to parry each thrust. So things stood, with daily skirmishes in force and artillery duels and cavalry raids, until the morning of June 27. On that date occurred the most ferocious of all the Kennesaw fighting, the official Battle of Kennesaw Mountain. It was a battle that will forever hold open a bright page in history as the one which brought luster to the valor of all-American soldiery, North and South.

That morning Sherman made a mass assault on Johnston and was repelled everywhere with shocking losses to the North. The attack was in two great waves—by the armies of McPherson and Thomas, assisted by cavalry.

McPherson's Blue veterans fought their way clear up the face of "Little Kennesaw." But there they were met with a concentration of rifle and cannon fire that staggered them backward, badly riddled. Thomas's deep wave of blue rolled against the heights just to McPherson's right. So far, no farther. The vaunted Army of the Cumberland could not stand up under the murderous fire of the entrenched Confederates.

An entire regiment of Federals, down below, charged into a line of Confederate rifle pits. These Union soldiers went down, rank on rank, line on line, wave on wave. They fell in sixes and eights, abreast, in tens and twenties, like grotesque, straw-stuffed blue dummies on some queer shooting-gallery contraption that moved the dummies toward the marksmen.

But the Blues came on. Nothing apparently could stop them. For upwards of an hour they advanced, row on row. The slaughter was ghastly, front rank going down, second rank going down, third rank going down. The riflemen in the pits had a moment to fall back to their main defense trenches farther up the mountain. There the killing began all over again. The Blues—middle-aged men from Northern cities and farm boys from Iowa and Nebraska and Wisconsin fought to the bayonet point, to the smoking cannon mouth. They fought to the very parapets and died sagging against those embankments, their arms flung outward like exhausted and collapsed runners. Behind those breastworks, middle-aged men from Southern cities and farm boys from Alabama and Texas and Mississippi and Georgia kept loading, aiming, and firing.

But the most powerful assault of the day of the main battle was made by a corps of the Army of the Cumberland. "Fighting Joe" Hooker was "refused," the military term for being held out of line in reserve, for the moment. This massive Cumberland attack was aimed at the positions held by Cleburne and Maj. Gen. B.F. Cheatham, just south of the big mountain.

On came the Cumberland Blues, several lines deep. Their bayonets glistened in the morning sun, the regimental colors fluttered in a light breeze. Their way lay through a woody area and a thick tangle of underbrush.

Behind their breastworks the Confederate sharpshooters waited grimly. Not a trigger was squeezed until the advancing Federals were within ten paces of the breastworks.

Then from "Cheatham Hill," as the position was known, came an appalling fire from all along the Confederate line. The air was a sheet of flaming iron, a blizzard of hot lead that tore through the Blue ranks, which fell, row on row. And still they came. The earth that had never before heard a cannon trembled with the onslaught; trees that had never seen a man die saw them die by the scores, the hundreds. At one or two points, entire advancing Federal columns went down like a board fence hit by a gale.

Sherman lost a general and his old law partner in that fatal thrust to slice through the Confederate middle on Kennesaw that day—Brig. Gen. Charles G. Harker and Col. Daniel McCook.

There was a moment's lull. Then from behind the Confederate trenches there arose a wild and fearful sound, the blood-curdling Rebel yell. In a crescendo never heard before, the yell smote the ears of blue-clad men dying or about to die on the slippery slopes of Kennesaw Mountain that June morning of 1864. Above the roar and smoke of battle it rang out piercingly again and again, and was taken up by men on higher ground until the very crags echoed with the exultant, terrifying cry. Its effect was magic. From ten thousand muskets above the lower battle line, volley after volley rang out, scattering death and carnage anew on the now horribly riddled blue forces below.

The sudden hurricane of death from rifle and cannon was too much for Sherman's heroic armies on the mountain. They retreated in wild disorder, leaving behind thousands who had died. (You will find the names of some of the dead and the states they came from on well-marked graves in Marietta National cemetery, twenty miles northwest of Atlanta.)

Beaten back, beaten downward, the Federal troops flattened themselves against the ground, still within range of that awful fire, seeking what shelter they could find. But lying flat, they still had spunk. Now and again they would pop up, in twos and threes, and pour back a defiant fire at the safely entrenched men in Gray.

Here on the sides of Kennesaw that twenty-seventh day of June, 1864, the awesome pageant of more than one hundred thousand men in blue trying to drive little more than forty thousand men in Gray off a mountain was presented. One hundred and fifty thousand American men on one mountain were fighting to the death.

While the assault was under way on Cheatham's Confederate line, a United States flag was planted right on the breastworks. A Confederate captain, armed only with a revolver, leaped upon the breastworks and wrested the flag from its moorings. The Federal color-bearer engaged him in a hand-to-hand struggle and shot the captain dead. Before he could plant the flag again, however, a dozen bullets ripped into the Union hero's body. He died, still clasping the flag tightly around the staff.

Chivalry still lived, too. The terrific cannonfire on the mountain set fire to the carpet of dry leaves and pine needles. The fire began to approach the section of the slopes where the ground was thick with Federal wounded, helpless and in danger of being burned alive.

Confederate Col. W.H. Martin of Arkansas mounted the breastworks and called to a colonel of the Federals that he would be willing to order a cease-fire while the conflagration was being put out. The offer was gratefully accepted, and the fighting ceased. The forest fire was extinguished by men on both sides, and the wounded were removed. Then the fighting was resumed fiercely all along the line.

The Battle of Kennesaw Mountain was one of the costliest Sherman was to fight in the entire war. While Johnston's losses were put at exactly 808, reports were that Sherman's losses in killed, wounded and missing were more than ten times that number.

The whole main Battle of Kennesaw Mountain lasted little more than three hours. It was over by 11 A.M. Sherman's generals withdrew their shattered divisions from nearly all points of assault, though sporadic skirmishing continued until July 3. Sherman glumly admitted that his rash venture, which had begun twenty-three days before, was a failure. He had killed a few hundred Confederates in order to gain not a foot of ground, and his own losses were colossal.

On June 29, Sherman wired Washington: "I am accumulating stores that will enable me to cut loose from the railroad for a time and avoid Kennesaw Hill, which gives the enemy too much advantage." A carefully worded understatement, but for Johnston, up on the mountain, it was to prove the handwriting on the wall. Sherman once again was preparing to throw a long snaking blue loop somewhere around the Confederates and head for Atlanta.

On July 3, Sherman's battered but still grand armies began to move out in force down the valley toward the Chattahoochee River.

This time the city of Atlanta was the immediate and only logical objective.

BIG BLUE WAVE SURGES
ACROSS PEACHTREE CREEK

Sherman's Georgia campaign must be understood. Sherman's armies simply had to retain possession of and stick close to the tracks of the Western & Atlantic Railroad or they were lost. That slender lifeline of iron rails connected directly to Sherman's major base at Chattanooga, thence between Chattanooga to Nashville and Memphis by other direct rail lines.

Every musketball, every powder charge, cannonball and shell, and every ounce of basic food supplies had to come over that railroad down to Sherman, now committed deep in the heart of the strongest segment of the Confederacy south of Virginia. Every replacement soldier likewise came by this vital link.

(In this history, Sherman's forces are roundly described at one hundred thousand men to Johnston's forty-two thousand. Actually, Sherman's strength varied from just over one hundred thousand at the start of the campaign at Dalton down to about eighty-one thousand at the end of the Battle of Atlanta. Betweentimes they rose to well above one hundred thousand. These represented replacements to cover his costly losses at Resaca, New Hope Church and Kennesaw, and in various skirmishes in force all along the route. Up to the Kennesaw Mountain siege, Johnston likewise had to depend on the W & A line for supplies and what few raw reinforcements could be spared from Atlanta and points southward in Georgia. Johnston's highest round fighting-force figure during the campaign was fifty-five thousand, and most of his reinforcements were green men and boys from the Georgia Militia or the Atlanta Home Guard.)

Behind this day-and-night struggle for retention of the precious W & A lay a drama to enrich history. Somewhere over in northern Mississippi, the brilliant Confederate cavalry raider, Maj. Gen. Nathan Bedford Forrest, was on his own with a small but tough force of veteran mounted fighters. Other bands of guerrillas lurked in the moss-shrouded swamps of Mississippi, or along the hills and ravines of Alabama and Tennessee, ready at a moment's notice to swoop in and cut rail lines, blow up bridges and attack the constant trickle of Union reinforcements on their way to bolster Sherman's losses in Georgia.

Meanwhile, a tragic cloud darkened the drama. It, too, was connected with the railroad in back of Sherman. But chiefly it concerned petty politics and personal vanities and grievances.

Up in Richmond, Jefferson Davis, the Confederate president, undoubtedly was a sick man. Historians describe him at this period as wishy-washy, fretful, "peevish as a woman." He rankled under a delusion that Johnston was spitefully refusing to obey orders to make a stand and fight Sherman. He burned up the wires to Atlanta, demanding to know this and that. He demanded to be advised at once of every strategic step Johnston intended to take. Johnston did not comply, probably for one of two reasons: either Johnston himself did not know sufficiently in advance what his next moves were to be (which is hard to believe when you look at his record of preparations during his famous retreat) or Johnston feared—with good justification—that Jeff Davis unwittingly would "leak" the information where it could get back to Sherman. Davis did have a weakness for newspaper interviews. It had been Johnston's experience that these interviews invariably appeared within a few days in one or more of the Atlanta newspapers, upon which Sherman depended almost wholly for his military information. Meanwhile, at Richmond, Davis was daily being harangued by Southern senators and congressmen and by Braxton Bragg, who had been relieved at Chickamauga and who still squirmed under the ignominy of his narrow escape there. They all clamored for Johnston's removal. "Put someone in command who will make a fight," they demanded. "Give us a general who won't retreat."

Thus the behind-the-scenes drama was unfolding, approaching its red-hot climax as Sherman, on July 3, 1864, made his next move on the great Georgia chessboard—his drive on Atlanta.

The guns of Kennesaw had fallen silent. But to Atlantans there was a strange, ominous feeling in the hot sultry air the morning of July 20, 1864. Out along Peachtree Creek they were fighting a pretty stiff battle; but in Atlanta things were unusually quiet.

Just before noon, the far, hollow sound of a single cannon broke the stillness of the little city. A Union gun had opened fire. At the corner of Ellis (then called East Ellis) and Ivy streets, a golden-haired little girl toddled out onto the dusty road in front of her parents' home, followed by a frisking puppy. Overhead a shell shrieked with a queer locomotive sound. There was a geyser of red clay and dust, an almost muffled explosion. The parents of the child ran out onto their front porch. Sprawled on the rim of a big dirt crater in the road was their little girl. Nearby lay the puppy; both were still, both quite dead. . . . They were the first to die in Atlanta under the siege guns of General Sherman.

Before he retired from Kennesaw Mountain on July 2, Johnston had taken precautions against being flanked. On June 28, his own engineers, assisted by detachments from the Georgia Militia and crews of slaves recruited from in and around Atlanta, had dug and fortified two lines on the north side of the Chattahoochee River, ten miles northwest of Atlanta.

The first of these defense lines crossed the W & A tracks at Smyrna on a ridge running northeast and southwest that about three miles southwest of Smyrna curved southward, following the meandering line of Nickajack Creek, a Cobb County stream that flows into the Chattahoochee River between the Old Mayson Turner Road and Green's and Howell's Ferry roads. The second line, nearer the river itself, extended from the general vicinity of the old Montgomery Ferry Road, where the Bankhead Highway now crosses the Chattahoochee.

Sherman now was maneuvering in force and with determination. On July 4, he advanced his troops to such an extent that Johnston decided to withdraw to his new river line. That defense

CROSSING THE CHATTAHOOCHEE—Union infantrymen and artillery moved toward Atlanta in pontoon boats like this one. (Library of Congress photo)

line was characterized by Sherman as "the best line of field entrenchments I have ever seen."

At this juncture, Sherman suddenly decided against any hasty move upon Johnston's Chattahoochee line. Instead, he ordered the cavalry division of the Army of the Ohio, under Stoneman, to proceed downriver and reconnoiter around Sandtown, Campbellton, and points to the south.

At the same time, McPherson's Army of the Tennessee was ordered to keep the Mayson-Turner ferry protected while another division of Stoneman's cavalry, under Brig. Gen. Kenner Garrard, was sent upriver to capture Roswell and Bolton. Johnston stayed put.

Only July 5, Garrard's cavalry division reached Roswell. There it found that Johnston's everywhere-at-once cavalry veteran, Joe Wheeler, already had burned the bridge across the river. Nettled, Garrard gave the order to burn all buildings and factories in Roswell. One of the factories thus burned was a small woolen mill which, for some reason, flew a French flag from a pole atop the factory. In Garrard's behalf, it should be recorded that he spared the finer old homes in Roswell.

Sherman's reply to Garrard's report on the Roswell situation throws a revealing light on the Union army chief's record of callous treatment of conquered citizens. In a message to the cavalry general, Sherman order him to "arrest all people, male and female, connected with those (Roswell) factories, no matter what the clamor, and let them foot it, under guard, to Marietta, whence I will send them by cars (railroad) to the North . . . . The women will make a howl. Let them take along their children and clothing, provided they have the means of hauling it or you can spare them. We will retain them until they can reach a country where they can live in peace and security." About four hundred Roswell citizens thus were uprooted from the only homes they had ever known, taken to Nashville, thence sent to Indiana. Many of them never saw Georgia again.

On July 7, the Federals began crossing the Chattahoochee, away from Johnston's fortified positions. Schofield's Army of the Ohio was first, crossing at Sope Creek, about midway between Powers Ferry and Johnsons Ferry. The crossing by the Twenty-third Federal Corps made it necessary for Johnston to abandon his dug-in

41

LT. GEN. JOSEPH WHEELER—Johnston's everywhere-at-
once cavalry commander. (Library of Congress photo)

positions north and west of the river and to pull in to the Fulton County (Atlanta) side.

Johnston, therefore, on the night and early morning of July 9-10, threw his army across the W & A bridge, which he then burned. He sent Joe Wheeler's cavalry above and that of Jackson below to watch for further moves by the enemy. Johnston proceeded toward Atlanta on the Marietta road, halting at a point on what is now West Marietta Street to establish headquarters and study his next move.

On Sunday, July 10, Sherman's only known Atlanta spy, boldly identified in reports as J.C. Moore, reported the goings-on in Atlanta. The city, he reported, was in a turmoil. Many citizens were leaving their homes, traveling southward and eastward. Almost all were taking their slaves or servants with them. A large area east of Atlanta was a vast concentration of army wagons, and a huge amount of machinery used in the manufacture of munitions already was en route to Augusta . . . . The spy Moore reported: "I have just left General Johnston's Headquarters . . . . They are at a small white house three miles this side (northwest) of Atlanta, on what is called the Atlanta and Marietta road . . . . Saw Mrs. Johnston and other ladies at General Johnston's headquarters yesterday. They seem to be having a jollification."

Meanwhile, Sherman was busily preparing to move against Atlanta via Decatur, six miles to its east. His engineers were rebuilding the W & A trestle across the Chattahoochee, and on July 12, this job appeared about complete. Two days later, Sherman ordered Thomas's Army of the Cumberland to cross the river at Powers Ferry or Paces Ferry. Schofield's Army of the Ohio was ordered to move toward Buckhead. McPherson's Army of the Tennessee was to come up abreast of Schofield so that the entire Federal armies formed a vast half-moon behind Nancy Creek.

Then on Sunday, July 17, all of Sherman's armies were well across the Chattahoochee, poised for a well-planned mortal blow at Atlanta.

During those fateful few days, a distinguished visitor arrived in Atlanta from Richmond—Lt. Gen. Braxton Bragg, the man "Dutch"

POLITICAL SKULLDUGGERY—Lt. Gen. John B. Hood (left) went over the head of his commander, General Johnston, and delivered a report critical of Johnston to Brig. Gen. Braxton Bragg (right). This

led to what some described as one of the worst Confederate blunders
of the war.   (Library of Congress photo)

Longstreet had saved the previous autumn at Chickamauga, the man relieved of his command and given a post in the Confederate capital as "military adviser" to President Jefferson Davis. He was officially on a "tour of inspection," with orders to report directly to President Davis.

There now ensued a bit of political skulduggery that was to result in one of the worst blunders of the entire War Between the States. Lurking in the shadowy background was the brooding John B. Hood. Disgruntled, dissatisfied with Johnston's caution, Hood committed the unpardonable military sin. He went over the head of Johnston and made a direct critical report of his superior to Braxton Bragg.

Hood wrote Bragg charging that Johnston was incompetent. He listed examples, mainly centering on the backward march from Dalton. Bragg immediately telegraphed President Davis a dark and gloomy picture of the Atlanta situation. Back came a wire from Davis directed to Johnston, in which the president of the Confederacy issued what amounted to an impossible ultimatum. He demanded immediate and full details of Johnston's present plan of campaign—such details "as will enable me to anticipate all events." Johnston, perhaps angered, certainly humiliated, delayed his answer.

That same night, Johnston and a few of his staff officers were discussing the situation at headquarters. The day had been blistering and dusty, but now a soft wind with some coolness in it blew over the outskirts of the city. Outside headquarters, a regimental band was trying to cheer up "Old Joe." They had played "My Old Kentucky Home," "Bonnie Blue Flag," and other popular airs, and were whooping it up with "Dixie" when Maj. Charles W. Hubner, Johnston's chief of telegraph, rode up and handed Johnston a telegram. Johnston carefully read the telegram and went pale. It was the order from Jeff Davis relieving him of command and placing the fate of Atlanta and Georgia in the hands of the hotspur Hood.

Johnston's general staff, on hearing the news, were outraged. They threatened to resign in a body. Cooler heads sought a compromise; they got together and, with Hood reluctantly concurring, sent a wire to President Davis urging him to reconsider.

46

Davis refused. Hood requested Johnston to remain in supreme command until the afternoon of the next day, July 18. Johnston consented.

An excerpt from a letter written July 18 by a Mississippi lieutenant to his wife read: "Hood is the most unpopular Genl in the army & some of the troops are swearing they will not fight under him. Brig. Genls Cols & company officers have been called together to forestall anything like an outbreak. Maj. Genls & Brig & all regret that Johnston is gone. Johnston has made himself very dear to the soldiers."

On the day Johnston was relieved of command, Sherman set up his headquarters—the first of many in the Atlanta struggles—a short distance from the present site of the Crossroads Primitive Baptist Church at North Powers Ferry Road and Mount Vernon Highway. Here are his orders for July 18:

"Thomas to occupy Buckhead and ridge between Nancy Creek and Peachtree and all roads toward Atlanta as far as Peachtree Creek.

"Schofield to occupy Peachtree Road where Cross Keys Road to Decatur intersects.

"McPherson to move toward Decatur and Stone Mountain and destroy sections of the Georgia Railroad." (These two points are six and sixteen miles, respectively, east of Atlanta.)

That night, July 18, 1864, Sherman spent at what is now the Peachtree Golf Club, at 4600 Peachtree Road.

Sherman was increasingly nervous about the Georgia Railroad. From Virginia, the day before, Grant had telegraphed him that Lee was toying with the idea of sending twenty thousand of his own badly needed men to Johnston's aid via Wilmington, Charleston and Augusta. Such a transfer of troops had been done before, under Longstreet, resulting in a heavy defeat for the Union at Chickamauga. It could be done again. The railroad had to be torn up.

Therefore Sherman sent the Sixteenth and Seventeenth Corps of McPherson's army from Roswell to Decatur, capturing that little town, and then sped the Fifteenth Corps on eastward to strike at Stone Mountain and cut the Georgia Railroad there.

47

Meanwhile, he moved the Fourth Corps to Buckhead, while the Union Fourteenth and Twentieth Corps marched southward from Paces Ferry along Paces Ferry Road and Howell Mill Road to Peachtree Creek.

Johnston, the day before he was relieved of command, had anticipated Sherman's moves. He accordingly had established a strong entrenched line just south of Peachtree Creek, thus putting a stream in his front instead of at his rear, as he had done in retreating to the Chattahoochee from Kennesaw.

The new Gray defense line began at a point on the W & A Railroad about two miles from the river and extended eastward for six miles. This Confederate line crossed the high ground in what is now Crest Lawn Cemetery, Howell Mill Road, the lowlands of Tanyard Branch (also known as Shoal Creek), crossed Peachtree Road at Spring Street, the valley of Clear Creek, and at the present intersection of North Highland Avenue and Zimmer Drive turned south, paralleling Highland and Moreland avenues until it reached the Georgia Railroad near the present Moreland Avenue crossing. From this point the line extended roughly south and southeast to the present East Atlanta business section at Glenwood and Flat Shoals avenues.

On July 19, Federal General Howard sent a division down Peachtree Road from Buckhead to make a crossing. "Fighting Joe" Hooker sent two Union divisions to the present Northside Drive crossing of Peachtree Creek. Maj. Gen. John M. Palmer's entire Fourteenth Union Corps of three divisions tried to cross the creek at Howell Mill Road, but all were beaten back.

Hood, now actively in command, had fought hard against all these attempts of the Union armies to cross Peachtree Creek. However, on July 20, Palmer hammered his way across the creek farther downstream, and by noon of that same day one division of the Union Fourth Corps had reached the high ground where Brighton Road now runs into Peachtree Road. A division of the Union Twentieth Corps then battled its way across the Peachtree Creek bridge and swung to join the Union Fourth Corps division on what is now Collier Road, then just a wooded country path. Other Federal divisions linked up the Blue line westward, extending it to beyond Moore's Mill Road, near the present Atlanta waterworks pumping station at the Chattahoochee River.

By noon of July 20, the entire Federal line (except McPherson's army, which was at Decatur and Stone Mountain) faced southward. The invaders presented an almost unbroken Blue wave along the higher ground of the present Collier Road. On detail, with firm orders to hold the sector known locally as Tanyard Branch at Collier's Mill, was Col. Benjamin Harrison, later to become the twenty-third President of the United States.

That morning, Sherman moved his headquarters, setting up now in a tent at the northwest intersection of the present North Decatur and Briarcliff roads, at the time and for many years to be known as "Old" Williams Mill Road.

Then it was that Hood, making every effort to meet Jeff Davis's telegraphed demands, made the first of three fateful attacks on Sherman's grand armies—but he tarried from noon to 4:30 P.M. for a reason known only to himself. That slight delay gave General Thomas time to put his Federal troops in position to meet the assault.

Confederate Gen. A.P. Stewart, now commanding the dead Polk's corps, sent two divisions outside Atlanta's outer defenses; General Hardee threw three divisions—holding back Cleburne's—and the divisions of Maj. Gens. W.B. Bate, W.H.T. Walker and Brig. Gen. George Maney moved out—Bate along Clear Creek just north of the present Piedmont Park; Walker into Collier's woods along Peachtree Road; and Maney through the thickets just west of Peachtree Road. W.W. Loring joined in the Confederate assault, his own division holding the hill now known as Loring Heights, and Maj. Gen. Ed C. Walthall along Howell Mill Road.

The Confederate mass assault struck the Union line squarely across Peachtree Road at Brighton Road. In this action, Confederate Maj. Gen. C.H. Stevens was killed. Loring hammered at Col. Benjamin Harrison's Union forces at the Collier Mill and at another Federal division between the mill and the present Northside Drive. The Confederates under Walthall charged a Federal division in and behind a deep gully at what is now Norfleet Road. The attack by Walthall was so spirited it nearly split two barricaded Blue divisions, but the Union line rallied and held. All along the line of assault the Confederates were hurled back with fearful losses.

The Confederate toll in the Battle of Peachtree Creek was indeed terrific. On his first try at direct assault, Hood was severely beaten and should have learned his lesson there. But he was to try again and again. The Confederate losses on July 20, 1864, at Peachtree Creek stood at 4,796 as compared to only 1,710 for the Federals.

(Today a monument in marble stands at the spot where the Battle of Peachtree Creek began—at Peachtree and Brighton roads, across from Piedmont Hospital.)

BATTLE OF ATLANTA LOST
AFTER EPIC NIGHT MARCH

Notwithstanding that the Federals now held the vital W & A Railroad to the north and had cut the Georgia Railroad to the east, Atlanta on the morning of July 22, 1864, stood in no real danger of being taken. The city's irregular circle of fortifications made it one of the most strongly protected cities on earth at that time. Sherman did not entertain the slightest notion of sacrificing his forces in a gamble to force the ten-mile circumference of high breastworks, redoubts, cannon emplacements, and rifle pits which for a year had been prepared for just such an eventuality. (As a matter of fact, not one Union soldier ever fought his way through those lines during the entire forty-two days that Atlanta was under the seige of Sherman.)

Because most Georgians are unaware of the tremendous defensive strength of Atlanta of 1864, it seems appropriate to describe the locations of the city's fortified lines which caused Sherman to hold back with singular caution where he had rushed a stronghold such as Kennesaw Mountain less than a month previously.

Roughly, the fortifications of Atlanta of 1864 were bounded on the north by the present Ponce de Leon Avenue, on the east by Boulevard, on the south by Atlanta Avenue and on the west by Ashby Street. Today, the homes, lawns, yards and streets of many Atlantans stand on hallowed ground where once an heroic and poorly equipped Gray army stood off a force more than twice its size and strength.

51

After the fall of Vicksburg, in July 1863, the Confederate War Department ordered Col. Lemuel P. Grant, chief engineer of the Department of Georgia, to begin fortification of the city. Grant, who later was to donate the land that became Atlanta's Grant Park, at once began setting up a line of defenses encircling the entire city. This line consisted of more than twenty strong redoubts on prominent eminences, all connected by high breastworks and deep rifle pits. The redoubts, breastworks, and rifle pits all were strongly revetted with heavy timber, and in most cases the outer sides of the breastworks were strewn with abatis (thousands of trees chopped down, their limbs sharpened into outward-pointing spears) and the formidable *chevaux de frise* (criss-crossed sharpened palings and stakes, the forerunner of modern barbed-wire entanglements). As completed, in April 1864, the city's fortifications also had deep trenches in front, making it suicidal for a foe to attempt to storm the banks.

In addition to the original circle of fortification, there were sections of the city in which a second, or outer, wall of breastworks, redoubts and rifle pits was thrown up. The entire area of present Grant Park was such an auxiliary fort. The ring of fortifications extended about a mile and a half on each quadrant, with Five Points as the rough center.

Atlanta indeed was a bastion when the crucial Battle of Atlanta was fought. (It should be remembered that the so-called Battle of Atlanta was not fought within the city limits of those days. Like the Battle of Peachtree Creek, its setting lay several miles outside the Atlanta of 1864.)

In a tent several miles east of Oakland Cemetery, a smartly uniformed Union major was annoyed as a corporal led in three scarecrow civilians carrying a flag made out of a white rag. They were an old whiskered man, a frail, careworn woman, and an emaciated boy of ten. They stood looking resentfully at the Yankee major, the dry skin drawn drum-tight over their starved faces.

"Well," snapped the major, "what do you people want?" The woman swallowed hard. "Our cow," she said dully. "Your sojers stole our cow. My baby's starvin', an' I ain't able to nuss him." The major's anger drained away. "What cow, lady?" he asked more gently. The woman pointed with her sharp chin. "Out there—we seen it. It's our onliest cow an' my baby's hungry." The major barked, a lieutenant appeared with a grin that instantly vanished. "Take these people out and feed them, Lieutenant," he said. "Give them some food to take back. When you do that, find that cow—and the men who took it." Around sundown the three scarecrows, toting two heavy canisters of food and leading a bony cow, trudged homeward through the hot dust. Cows have horns, the woman was thinking, but Yankee officers—well, not necessarily.

Now the weary chessmen in blue and in gray began to move on the grim board that was to be the awful Battle of Atlanta. The first moves actually were made even while the Battle of Peachtree Creek was raging, but every move now was to set up the fateful play for the big struggle.

On the morning of July 20, McPherson's Army of the Tennessee, centered around Decatur, began its move on Atlanta. The Federal Fifteenth Corps under General Logan left the courthouse square at Decatur and marched westward along Decatur's Atlanta Avenue, DeKalb Avenue, and the Georgia Railroad tracks, heading toward Atlanta.

Just behind Logan's Fifteenth Corps marched the Union Sixteenth Corps under General Dodge. The Seventeenth Corps meanwhile crossed to the south of the Georgia Railroad tracks and headed slightly southwest via the old Fayetteville Road.

All of these strong Federal units soon met stiff Confederate resistance along the present Whitefoord Avenue section. Meanwhile, the Federal Twenty-third Corps was hotly engaged along Briarcliff Road, and part of the Union Fourth Corps—not engaged at Peachtree Creek—ran head-on into a division of Confederate Gen. Ben. Cheatham's Corps. Wheeler's Confederate cavalry, dismounted, contested every inch of the advance of the Federal Seventeenth Corps along Moreland Avenue (now a continuation of Briarcliff Road), and at sundown on July 20, Wheeler rallied his foot cavalry to a strategic withdrawal to Leggett's Hill, where Flat Shoals and Moreland avenues now join.

The Federals concentrated on Leggett's Hill in determined assaults. Wheeler fought them off valiantly, and at midnight was

COL. LEMUEL GRANT'S FORTIFICATIONS—The crossed sharpened poles in the foreground were the Civil War equivalent of later-day barbed wire. These fortifications were at the head of Marietta Street guarding northwest Atlanta.
(Library of Congress photo)

POTTER'S HOUSE — This is a closer view of the white house opposite. It was occupied by Confederate sharpshooters, so was a special target for Federal artillery. (Library of Congress photo)

reinforced by Gen. Pat Cleburne's division of Hardee's corps.

July 21 dawned hot and stifling. To the north of the city, around Peachtree Creek, both Federals and Confederates, under a truce, buried their thousands of dead. Everything was comparatively quiet, except along Leggett's Hill on Moreland Avenue. There the fighting had resumed, hot and furious. Federal Brig. Gen. Walter Q. Gresham, whose division of the Seventeenth Corps had carried the brunt of the assault the preceding afternoon, had been wounded, and Gen. Frank P. Blair, Seventeenth Corps commander, was now personally directing the Federals. Brig. Gen. Giles A. Smith had succeeded to General Gresham's divisional command for the Federals. After a bitter struggle, the combined Federal forces drove Cleburne from Leggett's Hill. Nightfall found Sherman's left line securely dug in on what had been the right of Hood's main defense.

Out on the southeastern ramparts of the city's fortified line, a curious scene excited the interest of sweltering Confederate cannoneers. From a patch of woods to the left, twelve Union soldiers emerged in a crouch, apparently bent on rushing the big gun emplacement. Not a cannoneer moved. One hundred yards farther to the left, a fully manned Confederate rifle pit began to spit savagely. One by one the crouching blue figures straightened up, spun suddenly, and sprawled in the hot dust. One or two seemed to go into a sort of whirling dance before they toppled, as the .577-caliber slugs from the sharpshooter's Enfields ripped into them. Finally only one was left—a young man clad only in blue breeches, black shoes and a rakish scarlet forage cap. A big revolver stuck from his belt; he held a musket. His sweating torso gleamed in the scorching sun. He looked desperately to left and right, stood defiantly erect, rifle at the ready—a tense, thrilling portrait of a fighting man at bay. A dozen bullets sank into him. His musket fired as he crumpled, his face downward in the hot red dust . . .

Hood on July 21 reached what he thought to be a brilliant decision—a vast flanking movement to cut down Sherman's army at Decatur and his two big armies north of the city. Hood's plan was to send Hardee's corps on a night march southward in order to get around to the rear of McPherson's Army of the Tennessee in

Decatur and East Atlanta. This accomplished, he would send Cheatham's Corps in a general assault against Sherman's Armies of the Cumberland and of the Ohio simultaneously. It was a daring and dangerous gambit to split his inferior forces and try for a timed attack on vastly superior armies. Hood decided to throw the dice.

Having thus decided on this fateful move, Hood, to secure the safety of the city itself, withdrew all of his troops from the other defense lines on the morning of July 22 to the inner fortifications. Just a few hours earlier, during the night of July 21, Hood had ordered Wheeler's cavalry to attack the Federal left rear at Decatur in conjunction with Hardee's rear-flanking movement.

So it was that all during that night of July 21, Hardee's corps was on the move, from the present site of Peachtree and Spring streets, down Peachtree to Five Points. There the long, sweaty columns, tired and thirsty, came to a pause.

Word quickly spread through the little city that Hood was abandoning Atlanta! The rumor caused brief panic. Looting of stores and warehouses began but was stopped by the Georgia Militia before it got out of hand.

After its brief pause at Five Points, Hardee's long column marched southward through the city by way of present Capitol Avenue (then called McDonough Road) on out past the present site of Federal Prison, proceeding nearly to South River. There Hardee swung sharply northeastward along the old Fayetteville Road near the present Atlanta Police Academy on Key Road, which runs southwest off Bouldercrest Road at Walker High School.

Meanwhile, Cleburne's division, which had fought hard all day along Moreland and Flat Shoals roads, had joined forces with Hardee at Capitol Avenue and Memorial Drive. They marched on and on in a sweltering night, suffocating with clouds of dust kicked up by the Gray army on the march. The narrow roads were jammed with cavalry, infantry, field artillery, supply wagons. All the men were suffering from thirst; there was no water.

In his planning, Hood had accepted a deceptive conclusion: Hardee could attack the Federals in East Atlanta at daybreak of July 22. But that hour found Hardee's almost exhausted soldiers far from contact with the Federal left—somewhere near South River, in fact. It was nobody's fault. They had no maps, the heavily wooded country was totally unfamiliar to them, they lacked guides. Hardee of course knew the general direction of the Union forces but as July 22 dawned, it was essential that guides be enlisted to lead the Confederates to McPherson's positions.

Two guides were finally found. Both were badly frightened and reluctant. But they consented to lead Hardee and Generals Cleburne and W.H.T. Walker on a northward trek along the Fayetteville Road. Cleburne and Maj. Gen. George Maney soon took the left fork which led to East Atlanta over the present Bouldercrest Drive. Generals Walker and William B. Bate kept to the right along the Fayetteville Road. Wheeler, riding for Decatur, held to that same road. It was to prove a deadly mistake.

Walker's division swung northeastward at about where Wilkinson Drive now joins Glenwood Avenue. They soon were bogged down in a section known as Terry's Mill Pond. Walker, a man with an explosive temper, became infuriated with his guides, threatening to have them shot for suspected treachery. He insisted on proceeding along a route the guides had warned him not to take. Presently, on a slight rise of ground, Walker, still fuming, reined his horse and put his field glasses to his eyes to see what lay ahead. For him it was death, in the form of a Union picket concealed in the woods nearby. A trigger was squeezed, and Walker pitched from his mount.

The time was exactly noon. The Battle of Atlanta was about to begin.

Because there had been considerable shifting of the Federal lines during the night of July 21 and the next morning, Hardee's long and tiring night march failed in its purpose of surprising the Federals in that sector. General Thomas's Army of the Cumberland now lined up at Tenth Street, facing the Confederates along Ponce de Leon Avenue and what then was called West North Avenue (now North Avenue). A division of Dodge's Sixteenth Corps was hurriedly transferred from where Candler Park now is situated to the left of Blair's line in East Atlanta (Leggett's Hill on Moreland Avenue). This Federal division, under command of Brig. Gen. Thomas W. Sweeney, was hotfooting it along the present Clay Street a few minutes after noon and reached Memorial Drive at the very split second Confederate General Bate and Maj. Gen. Hugh Mercer (who immediately had succeeded the dead General Walker) dashed forward to lay into Blair's Federals on Leggett's Hill.

This sudden and unexpected appearance of the Federals under Sweeney and of the Confederates under Bate and Mercer was like two big men colliding as they round a corner. It set off the first clash of the actual Battle of Atlanta, and for more than two hours a Federal battery poured shells and solid shot into Bate's and Mercer's weary troops.

Meanwhile, Cleburne's and Maney's Gray divisions had surged up Flat Shoals Avenue and hammered hard at the flank of the Union division under Maj. Gen. Giles Smith. The fighting here was hot and furious. Cleburne's men stormed and captured the entire Sixteenth Iowa Regiment, got in the rear of Giles Smith's main line, captured a Federal battery, and maneuvered so that for more than a solid hour the forces of the Federal General Smith were caught in a murderous simultaneous attack from front and rear. This two-sided inferno proved too hot for the Federals, and Smith's forces were driven from their breastworks. They retreated to Leggett's Hill, joining their line on the right to that of Brig. Gen. Mortimer D. Leggett, the Federal officer for whom the hill is named.

On the afternoon of July 22, Sherman's headquarters was moved from the house at North Decatur and Briarcliff roads to a large two-story white frame house on top of a hill from which most of Atlanta's fortifications could be viewed. The new headquarters was situated on what is now Cleburne Avenue, just off North Highland Avenue.

One of the first visitors to Sherman's new headquarters was Maj. Gen. James Birdseye McPherson, the young and brilliant commander of the hard-hitting Army of the Tennessee. They discussed tactical matters briefly, chatted informally about the new Confederate commander Hood, whom both knew personally, and talked a bit on personal matters.

Whether the handsome McPherson mentioned to Sherman the latter's often-given promises of a leave of absence so that McPherson could go to Baltimore and marry the woman to whom he was engaged is a matter of conjecture. The engagement had been of long duration, and McPherson enjoyed the personal and almost paternal regard of Sherman. A coming marriage may well have been mentioned on that fateful early afternoon of July 22.

With only one aide and his signal officer, McPherson now galloped toward his lines. At the Georgia Railroad near Moreland and DeKalb avenues, the young general and his companions ate lunch under a cluster of shade trees. Suddenly they heard an unusual burst of gunfire from the direction where McPherson's troops were supposed to be. McPherson sent his aide away with oral orders, mounted his horse and inspected his lines through his glasses. He saw with dismay that his left flank was being seriously bent by a Confederate rear assault.

McPherson paused, turned in the saddle and gazed northward. Was he looking, in fancy, back to the little town of Clyde, Ohio, where he had spent such a happy boyhood? Was it toward Baltimore, where waited the woman he loved? One long look northward. Then, spurring his horse, he rode for the bend in the Union left.

Passing in the rear of a division of his own Sixteenth Corps, he galloped directly into an advancing line of Pat Cleburne's Gray troops. They shouted for him to surrender, but McPherson either did not hear or chose to ignore the order. A musketball tore through his lungs. So died McPherson, thirty-five years old and one of the most capable Union generals. Today a monument—a huge cannon embedded breech-down in granite, muzzle pointing skyward—stands at the intersection of McPherson and Monument avenues. Likewise, Ft. McPherson, headquarters post for the U.S. Army's Forces Command, memorializes his name and valor.

Sherman temporarily gave McPherson's command to Maj. Gen. John A. Logan. Five days later he gave permanent command to Maj. Gen. Oliver O. Howard. This so incensed "Fighting Joe" Hooker, who once had commanded the famous Army of the Potomac and who had been badly outgeneralled in Virginia by the late Stonewall Jackson, that he summarily resigned his own command, the Twentieth Corps of the Army of the Cumberland. Hooker was replaced as Twentieth Corps commander by Brig. Gen. Alpheus S. Williams on a temporary basis.

All this time the Battle of Atlanta was flaming with increasing fury. Pat Cleburne's Confederates desperately threatened Giles

MAJ. GEN. JOSEPH "FIGHTING JOE" HOOKER—When General
Sherman gave McPherson's command to Maj. Gen. John Logan, Hooker
became so incensed he resigned. (Library of Congress photo)

Smith's Federals on Leggett's Hill. The "hill" became a veritable carnage of slaughter. Having lost the position the day before, Cleburne was determined to retake it. There ensued close fighting with bayonet and clubbed musket and even shrapnel and grapeshot at a few paces distance. Huge holes were torn in the Confederate masses.

To add to the general confusion, an inadequately coordinated attack by Cheatham's Confederate corps failed. Sundown found Leggett's Hill still in possession of the Blues.

Meanwhile, heavy action had broken out around the unfinished brick home of George M. Troup Hurt on a knoll at the present site of the East Atlanta Primitive Baptist Church on DeGress Avenue. Then came Cheatham's forces in a line assault on the Federal Fifteenth Corps. Cheatham stormed down the Georgia Railroad tracks and met the Blue forces at about where DeKalb and Moreland avenues now intersect.

Cheatham's forces cracked the deep Federal line asunder at the Hurt house, and captured the DeGress battery of five twenty-pound Parrott guns. But the captors could not change the guns' positions since the Federal battery, seeing capture was certain, slaughtered all the horses used to maneuver the heavy cannon. Later that afternoon, General Logal sent in three Federal brigades, which restored the Union line at the unfinished house (shown prominently today in the world-famous Cyclorama painting in Grant Park).

Joe Wheeler, the old cavalry warhorse, enjoyed one of the few Confederate victories that day. The Gray cavalry chieftain arrived at Decatur via the Fayetteville Road that morning and found strong entrenchments of Federals on the south and east of the town. After a furious assault, his dismounted cavalrymen drove the Northern soldiers away from the courthouse square. He pursued them through and on out of town, a considerable distance to the north, taking several hundred prisoners, a big gun and many provisions. But even this minor victory was short-lived. Later Wheeler was forced to retire from Decatur when Hardee, hard-pressed in Atlanta, summoned his help.

It was another disheartening Confederate defeat. For all their determined fighting, their courage in the face of overwhelming odds, the Southerners lost the day—Hood's second major defeat in

BRIG. GEN. JAMES B. McPHERSON—A favorite of
General Sherman, McPherson was killed while trying to
reach his embattled troops near Moreland and
DeKalb avenues. (Library of Congress photo)

two days. The Confederates at nightfall retired within the city's still impregnable fortifications, but the losses were staggering: seven thousand for Hood, two thousand for Sherman.

Each side lost a general: Walker for the South and McPherson for the North.

The City of Atlanta was still intact. But its manpower defense had been almost shot to pieces.

EZRA CHURCH AND JONESBORO
FALL; ATLANTA EVACUATED

The Confederate army, though sorely battered, was by no means trapped inside Atlanta's fortifications. Weakened considerably, Hood's army still constituted a real and dangerous threat to the major objective of Sherman's three grand armies, which was to capture Atlanta and begin a devastating March to the Sea.

Hood still could rely on two railroads to bring in supplies and what reinforcements were left—that leading to Macon and the south, and the one leading to West Point and the west.

Everything now depended on those two railroads—or at worst, one of them. Both Hood and Sherman realized this, and Sherman lost no time in setting about to cut them both at the earliest moment.

The day after the Battle of Atlanta, Sherman began to shell the city with a vengeance. Withdrawal of Hood's weakened forces inside the city allowed the Union armies to press closer to Atlanta's ring of fortifications. Now the Federals began to erect forts and mount siege guns within easy range of the entire town. On Saturday, Sunday and Monday, July 23, 24 and 25, the invaders began raining explosive shells and red-hot cannonballs all over Atlanta.

Since shortly before the Battle of Kennesaw Mountain, thousands of Atlantans had begun to evacuate the city. On trains, in wagons, buggies, on horseback, on foot, they abandoned their homes and began a trek southward to Lovejoy's, Jonesboro, Forsyth, Macon, Milledgeville, or anywhere they could find temporary shelter. But in Atlanta there were many civilians who stayed, clinging to the fading hope that somehow Sherman would be pushed back. These now suffered the day-and-night inferno of incessant shelling.

On Tuesday, July 26, Sherman decided to strike at both remaining railroads where they entered Atlanta just below East Point. The orders went down the line, commands were snapped out, the Blue ranks began to move. The Union Sixteenth Corps on July 27 reached what is now Chapel Road and formed its lines along that road south of what is now North Avenue. That night, the moonlight gleaming on a forest of bayonets, the Union Seventeenth drew up behind the Sixteenth and at daylight on July 28 the Fifteenth Union Corps and the Seventeenth extended the line of the Sixteenth southward. To become the right wing of the main Army of the Tennessee, the Fifteenth had pulled up far down the West Lake Avenue area.

As the Seventeenth Corps marched by moonlight, a whisper ran through its ranks that brought goose pimples to the marching men of McPherson's famous corps. A man in the rear ranks of the vanguard glanced around, whispered to the man in front of him that *McPherson was up there, leading his toughened veterans in person!* The whisper ran through the whole line of marching men; but of course it was merely imagination. McPherson had been dead five days.

Now the Fifteenth Corps formed the right wing of the main Army of the Tennessee's line to the present Mozley Drive, then to old Green's and Howell's Ferry roads. There it swerved north-westward and ended on the upland ground just west of the present Sadie G. Mays Memorial Nursing Home on West Anderson Avenue. But before it linked up on this eminence it was detected by Confederate Brig. Gen. W.H. Jackson's cavalry division, and a sharp clash occurred. This was a forerunner of the Battle of Ezra Church—a little chapel in those times known as Ezra Methodist Chapel, situated in the present southeastern corner of Mozley Park on Martin Luther King Jr. Drive. (There are two historical markers on this site.)

Meanwhile, Confederate Lt. Gen. Stephen D. Lee had been called in to command Hood's old corps. And Hood, brooding but watchful, determined once more to attack the Federals. He would first wait for them to reach Lickskillet Road (now Gordon Road), leading to Adamsville. Having thus determined, Hood moved his Confederates out of the city once again, by Gordon Road, and formed his lines on and east of the present Westview Cemetery. Here Gen. Stephen Lee was placed in command of the corps Cheatham had led in the Battle of Atlanta, and Hood sent two divisions of that corps to block the Federal Fifteenth Corps at Lickskillet (Gordon) Road. Confederate Gen. A.P. Stewart was sent in with two divisions to back up General Lee.

So it was that on July 28, 1864, on the site of the present Mozley Park, there occurred shortly after noon the last of the direct major engagements having the city of Atlanta as the grand prize. This conflict was recorded in history as the Battle of Ezra Church.

When a red traffic light stops you on Ivy Street at Ellis, pause a moment to think. You are on the spot where the little girl playing with her puppy was blasted into eternity by a Federal shell on the morning of July 20, 1864. She was the first of the citizens of Atlanta to die. Others followed. Look at the jagged hole in the base of the old gas lamp post at Peachtree and Alabama streets where now stands the Five Points rapid rail station. It is, except for the jagged hole, just as it was on the bright hot morning of August 19, 1864, when good-natured Solomon Luckie, a black barber who enjoyed friendly acquaintance with the town's leading citizens, walked out for some fresh air and to listen to the booming guns to the north. He gave good-morning to two or three passersby. A terrific explosion occurred, and the lamp post swayed crazily. Solomon Luckie went down with a ghastly wound in his leg. A shell fragment, tearing through the lamp base, had struck him. They carried him gently into a nearby store, thence to the Atlanta Medical College. There Dr. Noel D'Alvigney amputated the leg and gave old Solomon some quieting morphine. He died two hours later. War, frightful war, had now come inside the little city of Atlanta.

The Battle of Ezra Church began in earnest where Gordon Road now joins Anderson Avenue. The advance Union skirmish line was pushed across the present Atlantic Coast Line Railway tracks to the higher ground on which Sadie G. Mays Memorial

Nursing Home stands today. But it was a maladroit move, badly bungled by the Confederates. It had begun as an all-out assault by General Lee's forces. Something—no one knows exactly what—went wrong. Troops failed to advance together. A battle order was wrongly interpreted. Confusion broke out. And what had begun as a powerful assault fizzled out with the Confederates tragically scattered.

Bad as it was, the Confederates gave the Union forces a bad time, forcing them to fight from behind logs and even benches torn from the little Ezra Chapel. But Hood's assault obviously had been ill-conceived and executed in a shoddy manner. Lee had failed, and General Stewart's troops came surging forward in a hopeless attack which continued throughout the afternoon. The attack was called off.

Confederate losses again were tragic—another five thousand men to Sherman's six hundred. Here was a third sorrowful example of both the undoubted courage and the recklessness of Hood ("all lion, none of the fox"). He had tried to throw back three grand armies of the United States with three tired and weakened Confederate divisions!

Now he realized that the game was almost up. He began feverishly a move to protect his two remaining railroads, throwing up still another line of trenches.

Meanwhile, Sherman began to tighten his Blue noose around Atlanta. He opened up with his heaviest artillery, shelling the city night and day. The tempo of the bombardment increased as the dry hot days of August enveloped the city. Sherman sent to Chattanooga for special rifled siege guns to train on the stricken town. Hood's official protest that the shelling of civilians was inhuman drew the sardonic reply from Sherman that even Hood must realize that "war is the very science of barbarity." Sherman shrugged off the protests with the contention that there were no civilians left in Atlanta. All the while there were many resident noncombatants caught in the inferno and now unable to get out.

Diaries of the period are scarce. But there are a few preserved notes on those terrible days in the city's history when Atlanta was on Sherman's condemned list. Wallace P. Reed, an Atlanta resident of that time, wrote:

"If any one day of the siege was worse than all the others, it was that red day (August 10) when all the fires of hell, and all the thunders of the universe seemed to be blazing and roaring over Atlanta . . . . About breakfast time a big siege gun belched forth a sheet of flame with a sullen boom from a Federal battery on the north side of the city (at about Eighth and Peachtree streets).

"The Confederates had an immense gun on Peachtree Street [this gun was embrasured on the present site of Crawford W. Long Hospital], one so large and heavy that it had taken three days to drag it to its position. This monster lost no time in replying to its noisy challenger, and then the duel opened all along the lines on the north and west. Ten Confederate and eleven Federal batteries took part in the engagement. Shot and shell rained in every direction. Great volumes of sulphurous smoke rolled over the town, trailing down to the ground; and through this stifling gloom the sun glared like a great red eye peering through a bronze-colored cloud."

More personally, Mr. Reed recalled the horror of the day with regard to specific persons and places:

"A shell crashed into a house on the corner of Elliott and Rhodes streets. The explosion killed Mr. Warren, the superintendent of the gas company, and his six-year-old daughter . . . . A woman ironing clothes in a house on Pryor Street between the Methodist Church (Candler Building) and Wheat Street (Auburn Avenue today) was struck by a shell and killed . . . .

"A young lady who was on her way to the Car Shed (now the site of Plaza Park at Pryor and Wall streets) was struck in the back and mortally wounded . . . . On Forsyth Street near Marietta, a Confederate officer was standing in the front yard, taking leave of the lady of the house, when a bursting shell mortally wounded him and the lady's little boy. The two victims were laid side by side on the grass under the trees, and in a few minutes both bled to death."

Old men and women, mothers left in the stricken city with their children, fled into cellars and "shebangs" dug into the sides of railroad embankments or other eminences—anywhere to get away from the awful bursting shells. Federal hot-shot furnaces all about the city heated solid cannonballs until they were a cherry red, rammed then into wet-wadded cannon, and slammed the incendi-

69

AN ATLANTA "SHEBANG".—Hundreds of these small caves were dug in and around Atlanta during the merciless shelling of the city. This one was at the Joseph Willis home in Cascade Heights.
(Drawing by Wilber Kurtz, Sr., Atlanta Historical Society collections.)

ary balls into the city, where they set fire wherever they came into contact with flammable substances. Sherman apparently had set out to batter Atlanta from the face of the earth.

Thousands of wounded soldiers lay for days in the open without anesthetics or other pain-killers. There was no morphine, no chloroform, no antiseptics to be had. Doctors were tragically scarce, but the older civilians and the women gave what aid they could to the wounded Confederates. When it was possible, the wounded were shunted off toward the south, on trains, in bullock carts, covered wagons and open drays.

Sherman had replied, in answer to Hood's protest against the shelling of civilians, that any shells that fell in the city were purely coincidental to the fighting on the outskirts. This is hardly borne out by the following order, dated Aug. 1, 1864, from Sherman to General Schofield: "You may fire 10 to 15 shots from every gun you have in position into Atlanta that will reach any of its houses. Fire slowly and with deliberation between 4 P.M. and dark . . ." This order is a matter of official record, and it was issued when the shelling had not yet reached its height. It was to grow worse daily.

Sherman's order to General Thomas on August 7 read: "Telegraph to Chattanooga and have two 30-pound Parrotts sent down on the cars, with 1,000 shells and ammunition. Put them in your best positions and knock down the buildings of the town. Slow progress here."

After the first days of terror-stricken hiding in cellars and "shebangs," Atlanta's citizens apparently became used to the ordeal. They began to creep out of their holes and go about the city when they had any business that carried them out. I.B. Pilgrim made a note to that effect, and the historian Thomas H. Martin wrote:

"Aug. 4th was the fifteenth day of the constant shelling of the city, yet on that day as before, women and children would walk along the streets as though there were no army within a hundred miles, and nearly, if not quite, two-thirds of the houses in the city were still occupied by the inhabitants, many of them the oldest people in the place."

71

Day and night, citizens were killed and maimed; day and night, fires broke out, and the little town's volunteer fire fighters had to drop what they were doing and rush to the scenes of the conflagrations. Yet Atlanta held, and the siege went on and the guns went on. The food stocks grew frightfully low, even for the defenders, and the civilian populace was reduced to starvation rations.

A shifting of the Federal forces after Ezra Church threw General Schofield opposite Confederate General Bate, who now held a position south of Sandtown (Cascade) Road. On August 6, Schofield charged against Bate's men, but Bate proved to be too tough to handle. One of the Union divisions then tried a flanking movement, and Bate, a student of Johnston's wary tactics, withdrew to the main Confederate fortifications.

It was then and there that Sherman, once and for all time, gave up the idea of a direct assault on Atlanta through the fortified lines. Until August 25 he moved only at night, trying to sneak up on the Confederate positions, shelling the city without letup; and he also probed daily to reach and cut the West Point and the Macon railroads, the only two remaining links to the outside world for General Hood. Confederate Cavalry Gen. Joe Wheeler beat him back.

On August 25, Sherman's big guns fell suddenly silent. It was the first day since July 20 that not a Federal shell fell on Atlanta. The town was a rubble of ruins, a dead city so far as buildings were concerned. The reason soon became apparent: Sherman was on the move once again.

Sending an entire corps to guard his supplies at the Chattahoochee River, he ordered everything he had left "far below Atlanta." This strategy should have been crystal clear—from points below Atlanta he could cut both the Macon and the West Point railroads. Also, for Hood to counteract these Federal moves, Hood would have to pull his shattered troops entirely out of Atlanta's impregnable breastworks.

Not until the West Point Railroad had been cut below East Point did Hood realize the significance of Sherman's move. Hood likewise learned that Sherman had stationed the entire Army of the Tennessee and a full corps of the Army of the Cumberland near Jonesboro. Now Hood had to move, and fast.

He did, sending two corps on August 30, under Hardee's general command (Hood's old corps, led by Cleburne, and Lee's corps). And at 3 o'clock on the afternoon of August 31, the Battle of Jonesboro began.

Cleburne and Lee smashed into the Federal Fifteenth Corps between Jonesboro and the Flint River. Cleburne was successful, driving a Federal cavalry division across the Flint; Lee's assault was ineffective. Then came disaster.

That same afternoon, Hood, learning that two Federal corps were at the village of Rough and Ready, saw in this a direct threat of assault on Atlanta from the south. Hood immediately ordered Lee's Corps from Jonesboro to East Point. This left the spunky Irishman, Pat Cleburne, to face what now had grown to six full Federal corps. The end was predestined. The Federals swooped down on Cleburne, capturing an entire brigade, nearly capturing Cleburne's whole corps. Cleburne beat a quick retreat to Lovejoy's Station.

Here was the Confederate situation when the sun went down on the last day of August, 1864: Hardee's Corps cut off at Jonesboro; Lee's Corps caught between; and Maj. Gen. A.P. Stewart's corps, with the Georgia Militia, inside the fortifications of Atlanta, protecting the city. The black news received by Hood that the Federals had cut the West Point Railroad connection caused him to decide that Atlanta could be held no longer. Without delay, Hood gave the order to evacuate the city. Atlanta was lost.

Hardee and Cleburne meanwhile had retreated to Lovejoy's Station. Lee's Corps marked time at the present intersection of Moreland Avenue and McDonough Boulevard. Hood ordered Lee to stay put and await orders; later he directed him to join Hardee and Cleburne at Lovejoy's.

The evacuation of Atlanta began at 5 P.M. on September 1, 1864. Hood and his staff left for Lovejoy's on the short stretch of the Macon Railroad still in his hands, followed by the Georgia Militia under Maj. Gen. Gustavus W. Smith. The last troops to leave the city were Stewart's Corps. Hood left a detail of cavalry behind with certain orders. By midnight most of the Confederate troops were out of the city, heading southward.

Hood's detailed cavalrymen then blew up eighty-one freight carloads of ammunition and seven locomotives on the tracks near

THE RUINS OF HOOD'S RETREAT—As Hood retreated from Atlanta, he blew up this rolling mill, seven locomotives and eighty-one boxcars loaded with Hood's abandoned ammunition. (Library of Congress photo)

the Confederate Rolling Mills (later Fulton Bag and Cotton Mills at the railroad underpass on Boulevard at Decatur Street). They then blew up the rolling mills and rode out of town to join their leader southward. The explosion, louder and more shocking than anything yet experienced in Atlanta, rocked the entire city and stunned the remaining citizens. Every building for a quarter of a mile from the vicinity of the ammunition blowup was demolished. Atlanta was a dead city. It was to be cremated, on Sherman's orders; but later.

Daylight brought a new period of terror for the citizens. They emerged from their houses in quiet, stunned groups, wondering what would happen now. The entire Confederate army was retreating southward. The little city was being fast overrun with stragglers, deserters, "poor white" riffraff, and half-delirious blacks on a rampage of newfound liberties. Stores were plundered, houses broken into and stripped of every vestige of furniture.

Mayor James M. Calhoun hastily called a conference with members of City Council and prominent citizens. They all met on horseback, at Peachtree and Marietta streets. Mayor Calhoun told the group a delegation must approach Sherman, officially surrender the city, and ask for military protection.

Meanwhile, Federal Maj. Gen. Henry W. Slocum, who had replaced "Fighting Joe" Hooker as Twentieth Corps commander, started units of his army toward Atlanta from the Chattahoochee banks. These units met the group headed by Mayor Calhoun, bearing a white flag. The mayor acquainted the captain of a Federal unit with his mission, and the civilian party was escorted to a larger Federal unit, the commander of which requested the mayor to put the surrender in writing. This done, the note was forwarded by courier to Federal headquarters, and Mayor Calhoun and his party turned and rode back to town.

Sherman was down at Lovejoy's, but he had heard the mighty explosions and correctly guessed that Hood was giving up Atlanta. Even then, the hard-bitten Sherman displayed the healthy respect he held for Atlanta's strong fortifications. He telegraphed General Thomas on the Chattahoochee: "Until we hear from Atlanta the exact truth, I do not care about your pushing your men against breastworks. Destroy the railroad well up to your lines. Keep

75

BOXCARS PILED HIGH WITH HOUSEHOLD GOODS — This was the last train to leave Atlanta in the evacuation. (Library of Congress photo)

THE END OF ATLANTA DEPOT — This is the same building (opposite page) after Sherman ordered it destroyed.

(Library of Congress photo)

skirmishers well up, and hold your troops in hand for anything that may turn up. As soon as I know positively that our troops are in Atlanta I will determine what to do."

By noon September 2, the entire length of Marietta Street was blue with Federal soldiers. Atlanta men and women watched them glumly, but small boys capered up and down the Union marching lines jeering and whistling "Dixie."

The first Federal troops to enter the city was a Massachusetts regiment, and the first act of its commanding officer, Col. Willian Cogswell, was to haul down the drooping Stars and Bars from the City Hall. He ran up the Stars and Stripes. This marked the first time the Union flag had flown over Atlanta since early in 1861.

On September 3, Sherman moved all his stores from Allatoona and Marietta into Atlanta, but decided for the present not to pursue the fleeing Hood. Next, Sherman chose his "permanent" Atlanta headquarters—the newest and finest home in the city. It stood on what now is the grassy corner of the present City Hall at Mitchell and Washington streets.

On September 7, on orders from Sherman, it was announced that all civilians be evacuated from Atlanta to Rough and Ready. From there Sherman would transport them as far south as Lovejoy's. Between September 11 and September 20, every Atlanta family was required to register for the move, and on the latter date the exodus was carried out—four hundred and forty-six families consisting of seven hundred and five adults and eight hundred and sixty children, accompanied by seventy-nine black servants left Atlanta. Only a handful of Union sympathizers were left in the city to keep company with the wildly hurrahing, rowdy soldiers in blue. As a Confederate stronghold, Atlanta was dead.

SHERMAN MARCHES TO THE SEA
IN A DRIVE TO "RUIN GEORGIA"

With Atlanta in his pocket, Sherman decided not to pursue or even attempt to interfere with the southward movement of Hood's beaten and retreating Confederates. This was no mere gesture of contempt on the part of Sherman, who centered his every plan now on what he had announced would be a "March to the Sea." But Hood was to keep Sherman uneasy, looking over his shoulder, for more than two months.

Hood's desperate plan was to result in one of the most absurd situations ever conceived in warfare, presenting as it did the spectacle of a beaten army marching almost directly back over the route of its defeat, leaving Sherman free to drive towards Savannah in a wide two-pronged advance which would leave barren a swath averaging forty miles in width from Atlanta to the beautiful city by the sea. Pointless though it appeared, there was a glimmer of sense to Hood's frantic plan. If he could circle around Atlanta and destroy the W & A northward, meanwhile capturing token Federal garrisons and destroying storehouses of supplies, then he might at long last catch Sherman in a cut-off condition that would make possible Hood's dream of ultimate victory. It was a long, long chance, and historians have poked fun at Hood's "crazy idea." It could have worked. But it didn't.

Meanwhile, there were two matters that require relating before either Hood or Sherman moved toward their respective destina-

79

tions: a particularly spectacular cavalry battle that raged all the way between the Jonesboro area and the outskirts of Macon, in which the Confederates scored their last major victory in Georgia; and the decision of Sherman to cremate the corpse of Atlanta.

The day before Atlanta was evacuated by the Confederate army, Sherman's cavalry raiders struck and cut the Macon Railroad four miles below Jonesboro. General Hood, however, still in a fighting mood, rushed infantry reinforcements to aid his cavalry under Gens. Wheeler and W.H. Jackson. Wheeler's hard-riding horsemen slashed viciously at the northern cavalry, thwarting a direct assault in force by the Federals on both Macon and Andersonville.

Sherman had readily concurred in a proposal by his cavalry leader, General Stoneman, to bring about the dramatic release of some thirty thousand Union prisoners held in the filthy Andersonville Stockade. Stoneman seemed particularly bent on his adventure, and there are those who say he was out for some glory-grabbing headlines in the northern press. Sherman also thought the idea a good one and, within limitations, told Stoneman to go ahead with the plan.

Whatever his motives, Stoneman discovered with a shock that Macon was no pushover, and Andersonville was out of the picture so far as a rescue was concerned. Confederate Maj. Gen. Howell Cobb, after a hasty conference with General Johnston—in that vicinity on his way to a new command in South Carolina—lashed out at Stoneman's division with such ferocity that the Federal cavalry chief decided to beat a quick retreat back toward Atlanta. He and his twenty-two hundred cavalrymen rode hard northward.

Meanwhile, Federal Maj. Gen. Edward M. McCook, with thirty-two hundred cavalrymen, ran into a veritable tornado of Confederate resistance at Newnan, being checked there until Wheeler's forces could ride up and launch an all-out assault. The Confederate cavalry at Newnan routed McCook's division and took two hundred prisoners, many horses, wagons and field guns. In this engagement the Federals had ten times the strength of the force under Wheeler, and at about this time up rode Jackson with his three hundred men. Wheeler assigned Jackson to guard the Union prisoners.

Maj. Gen. Alfred Iverson took up the pursuit of the fleeing Stoneman, overtook him twenty miles north of Macon, soundly defeated his division and captured General Stoneman along with three hundred of his command. The remainder of Stoneman's forces were scattered in wild disorder. Of the fifty-four hundred cavalrymen in Stoneman's and McCook's assaults, only five hundred of McCook's and a few stragglers from Stoneman's divisions ever returned—a Federal loss of about five thousand men.

Worn thin by the heavy fighting of June, July and August, the Federal armies now settled down to comparatively easy lives of enjoyment in captured Atlanta. Shanties of the blue-clad victors went up everywhere, the lumber coming from houses torn down all over Atlanta's residential areas. Yankee officers of field grade and higher took over the most pretentious dwellings left standing after the bombardment. Sherman not only strengthened the city's erstwhile Confederate ring of fortifications, but he also pulled them into a smaller circle. Strong picket lines were set out southward—almost to the camps of Hood near Lovejoy's. At about this time Sherman had his own personal intuition and some reliable information about Hood's "crazy" plan to snake around Atlanta, march northward, and hack away again on the battered W & A.

Sherman's hunch, if it were such, was correct. On September 18, Hood's ragged, hungry army began to move westward from Lovejoy's toward the Atlanta and West Point tracks. Confederate headquarters were set up at Palmetto. And a week later there occurred an event which must have sorely galled President Jeff Davis, now almost in daily touch with Hood.

Hood (sometimes accused of apple-polishing) had persuaded Davis to take the cars down from Richmond and give Hood's poor army a top-level pep talk. So to Palmetto, on September 25, came Davis, ostensibly for a conference with Hood. Accompanied by staff officers, Davis called for a review of all Confederate troops in Hood's command. It turned out to be an embarrassment for him. Hungry, in tatters, dog-tired, the hard-bitten remnants of Joe Johnston's once unbeatable Army of Gray all but refused to listen when Jeff Davis began speaking.

"Give us back old Joe!" they shouted in chorus. "We don't want a speech! We want Old Joe back!"

81

GENERAL SHERMAN AFTER CAPTURE OF ATLANTA — Astride his horse at one of the captured Confederate gun emplacements that ringed the city. (Library of Congress photo)

But Davis went ahead with his speech, foolishly publicizing the plans he and Hood had made for the march of Hood northward. Needless to say, this was all the confirmation Sherman needed. Contemptuously now, Sherman remarked on hearing Hood's plans, "If Hood will go on up to Tennessee, I'll gladly supply him with rations." And that was precisely what Hood intended to do. He was to go "up to Tennessee" and down to utter defeat and oblivion, taking his gallant, still-obedient legion with him.

Hood began his rambling roundabout move toward Tennessee on October 1. Thus, once again the historic old W & A Railroad between Atlanta and Chattanooga became the bone of contention. Once again the men in tattered gray marched into and through the towns and past the courthouses and churches with the old familiar battle names—Marietta, Big Shanty, New Hope Church, Allatoona. And once again Sherman was forced to move, this time out of Atlanta, all but his Twentieth Corps, which stayed behind to hold the ruined city.

Hood, meanwhile, wrested small triumphs, capturing mere squads of Federal pickets or stragglers. His men were for the most part sick and hungry, some almost naked from the waist down, many shoeless, all footsore. The weather turned suddenly cold. Food had become the daily object of life, for now this valiant army was reduced to a cruel subsistence not of corn meal and bacon but of what corn on the ear they could get, parched over campfires and crumbled by the men who beat the hard grain with rocks. By night they marched on, wolf-eyed with hunger, sick with dysentery and scurvy; they were mere skin and bones, and those who were mounted rode drooping, bony horses. These were men, many of them, who once had slept on canopied feather beds, had drunk buttermilk in the cool of the afternoon from sterling cups, had dined at groaning tables covered by snow-white napery, had eaten from Royal Derby china, and had drunk Madeira from heavy cut crystal. Many had known fine imported broadcloths and Irish linens as a matter of daily apparel. And the poorest who now marched in this weary, ghostly army had known far better living than they now endured, their sore gums sucking on crude parched corn, their lips swollen and black from biting off cartridge tips, some spitting out loose teeth like orange pips as they trudged along.

Hood succeeded in routing the Federal garrison at Allatoona, but only for a few hours, for Sherman had sent out a force that now was breathing down the Confederates' necks. Hood traveled too rapidly to do any telling damage, and from Resaca, scene of Johnston's victory of a few months previously, he swerved southwestward, crossing the Coosa River near Gadsden, Alabama, and thence proceeded northwest to Florence and Columbia. From there he drove hard to Spring Hill, Franklin, and Nashville, in Tennessee.

Franklin proved Hood's Waterloo, though he fought later at Nashville. The Battle of Franklin was fought November 30. Hood was bloodily beaten, losing six thousand men. In this battle he lost the gallant Pat Cleburne and five other generals: Adams, Carter, Strahl, Granbury, and Gist. All were killed.

Staggering from the Franklin debacle, Hood rushed headlong to final disaster. On December 15-16, at Nashville, his tattered little army suffered its final defeat of the war. Hood managed to lead his skeleton survivors down into Tupelo, Mississippi, where on January 3, 1865, he resigned command, turning what was left of his forces over to the still dashing Gen. Pierre Gustave Toutant Beauregard.

Broken in body and spirit, the big Kentuckian Hood—once the idol of his tall yellow-haired Texans, once the fearless Lion at Gettysburg and again at Chickamauga—could only wince as his ears caught the bitter parody on "The Yellow Rose of Texas" sung by his defeated marchers as they stalked into Tupelo:

> You may sing about your Beauregard,
> And sing of General Lee,
> But the gallant Hood of Texas
> Played hell in Tennessee.

Now the Union drummers beat the long roll, the buglers trumpeted all their strident messages for the refurbished northern armies in blue to shoulder arms and take to the saddle. Sherman was ready to begin his historic March to the Sea. On November 9, from Kingston, he issued orders dividing his armies into two wings—the right, under General Howard, the left under Maj. Gen. Henry W. Slocum. On November 12, he ordered the much shattered and repaired W & A Railroad, his sole line of communication, torn up all the way from Atlanta to Dalton. Thus, he crossed his Rubicon and committed his big armies to live off the land.

By November 14, Sherman had purged his forces of the weak, the wounded and the sick—all the unfits. Only the toughest would march to the Georgia coast. The two prongs numbered 62,204 officers and men, including 5,062 cavalry and 1,812 artillerymen. It had twenty days' supplies rationed out as well as a large number of cattle on the hoof sufficient to provide meat for forty days in the field.

On this date Sherman gave the fateful order to put the torch to Atlanta. This was done the night of November 14. When the fire burned itself out, only about four hundred out of five thousand dwellings and other buildings were left in the desolate city. The morning of November 15, the main bodies of Federal troops marched out of Atlanta. Sherman remained behind until the following day. Then, accompanied by his personal staff, an infantry and a cavalry escort, and a regimental band, Sherman mounted his horse and rode leisurely east on Decatur Street. In his departure, he paused only twice, and briefly—once to glance backward at the smoking wrecked prize he had captured at the cost of so much blood; the second, to gaze soberly at the wooded spot where his favorite, General McPherson, had been killed. Then he nodded curtly to a staff officer.

Commands rang out, the march was on. At this moment the accompanying band struck up the moving strains of "John Brown's Body." Men in the marching ranks took up the song, singing lustily, triumphantly, as the escort columns moved south. Erect in his saddle, William Tecumseh Sherman, unquestionably the most unwelcome visitor Atlanta was ever to experience, rode out of the blazing city.

Spreading out his columns to a width of more than forty miles, Sherman tore up every mile of railroad track, burned almost every station; but did not, as generally reported, put to flames every town he passed. His men looted town dwellings and farms of provisions and private property. Sherman's tough bummers, though under his orders to limit their seizures to necessary supplies, stole silver, jewelry, personal knickknacks; they bayoneted tapestried furniture,

ATLANTA BANK IN RUINS—This bank was destroyed by Sherman's troops, while buildings around it were spared.

(Library of Congress photo)

battered magnificent pianos and spinets; slaughtered cattle, stole and shot pigs and sheep and poultry in much the wild fashion of European vandals.

Sherman, in his official report to Generals Grant and Halleck, the latter chief of staff in Washington, said that he personally knew of no instances of murder or rape by his foraging bummers. But there were numerous verified instances reported in and along the route of his Savannah drive. In those same official reports, however, Sherman betrays his personal and official attitudes when he uses such expressions as "utter destruction of roads, houses and people," "make Georgia howl," "make a wreck of the road and of the country," "smashing things to the sea," "make the interior of Georgia feel the weight of war," and "ruin Georgia."

Most candid of Sherman's reports is that to Grant after his capture and investment of Savannah. This report shows, with unblushing clarity, that Sherman was cognizant of depradations outside the bounds of his winked-at orders. He said: "We have also consumed the corn and fodder in the region of the country 30 miles on either side of a line from Atlanta to Savannah, as also the sweet potatoes, cattle, hogs, sheep and poultry, and have carried away more than 10,000 horses and mules, as well as countless number of their slaves. . . . This may seem a hard species of warfare, but it brings the sad realities of war home to those who have been directly or indirectly instrumental in involving us in its attendant calamities."

As to rank and file, Sherman reported to Grant that they had been "a little loose in foraging, they 'did some things they ought not to have done,' yet on the whole they have supplied the wants of the army with as little violence as could be expected, and as little loss as I calculated. . ."

Sherman's own quotation marks around "did some things they ought not to have done" betrays a culpable knowledge existing between himself and his superior that his marauders had, indeed, gone beyond the limits of necessary warfare. But he chose publicly to contend otherwise.

Sherman's march to Savannah was easy. But he met some annoying resistance all along the way. There was no strong opposition, however. On his way he paid scant attention to Covington, but deemed it necessary to burn the station and a few

UNION SOLDIERS RIP UP RAILS — Before beginning his "March to the Sea," Sherman ordered all rail lines supplying Atlanta destroyed. (Library of Congess photo)

surrounding buildings at Madison. The Federals ran into some resistance in skirmishes at Clinton, East Macon and Griswoldville. The Griswoldville action took place November 20-21-22.

Action occurred just east of Macon November 21, and on November 25-26 he had to stand off Joe Wheeler's cavalry at and around Sandersville.

A heavier engagement was fought at Milledgeville, where on November 23 Sherman burned the state penitentiary and the state arsenal, ran the Union flag up the Georgia state Capitol and departed.

Fighting occurred November 27-28 at Waynesboro and Davisboro, and on November 29-30 there were heavy skirmishes at Louisville. Some plantations near Louisville were burned, but Sherman officially denied he ordered the fires.

December 1-2-3 saw the Federals in light action at Millen, where he burned the depot and hotel; and on December 4 a heavier engagement was fought at Waynesboro and Statesboro. On December 5 there was a lively scrap at the Little Ogeechee River at Buck Head Creek, Cypress Swamp, and the Bryant County courthouse.

Rolling southward on or ahead of schedule, the Blue armies fought a series of skirmishes at the Ogeechee Canal, between Eden and Pooler, and in the big Monteith Swamp. Nearing Savannah, a stiff action was fought December 10 near Springfield and almost on the outskirts of the seaport city. On that date, too, the Union forces captured the Confederate steamer *Ida,* and two days later seized the Confederate steamboat *Resolute.*

Now the tempo of the drive against Savannah itself began to quicken. On December 13, an almost full-scale battle for the capture of Ft. McAllister, guarding the city, was fought, resulting in a Union victory. The next day, Union naval units opened up on Forts Rosedew and Beaulieu on the Vernon River, and a heavy skirmish took place December 16 at Hinesville.

Under a flag of truce, Sherman sent in a demand to Confederate General Hardee, in charge at Savannah, demanding surrender of the city. Refusing, Hardee, who had been relieved at his own request after the Battle of Jonesboro, escaped from Savannah with about fifteen thousand Gray veterans. They made their way into South Carolina, where Hardee was given command of the South Carolina-Georgia department.

Savannah was completely invested by Sherman on December 21. The next day the Federal chief reported to Grant that Hardee "got his garrison across (the Savannah River) and off, on the Union plank road." Sherman reported to Grant that Savannah's citizens "mostly remain, and the city is very quiet."

So came to a close the bloody Georgia Campaign of 1864.

A century later Georgia was not to have recovered entirely from its gashing wounds of military might, or the lingering miasma of northern resentment of the determined effort of the Confederate army in Georgia to resist invasion. Sporadic fighting continued on into the spring of 1865, but Sherman's capture of Atlanta and his March to the Sea sealed the doom of the Southern Confederacy.

Of those upon whose shoulders fell the stars of command, many were to be revered in history and public acclaim. Some died the soldier's death, on the field. Most died prosaically, in bed. A bullet took the South's *beau sabreur,* J.E.B. Stuart, leading a cavalry charge, black-plumed hat held high. Stonewall Jackson went down in his glory as the result of a natural mistake of his own men. Fiery Pat Cleburne heard the wild Rebel yell ringing in his ears when he fell. Chivalrous McPherson rode heedless into his enemy's front lines, thinking perhaps of a fair face in Maryland. Even little George Custer, his service totally undistinguished in the war, blundered into final, fatal glory, dying to the war-whoop and bugle.

"Fighting Joe" Hooker deserved such a picturesque end, as did James ("Dutch") Longstreet and Grant and McClellan and Hood. But they died in bed. Lee died as he had lived, quiet and uncomplaining. But McClellan, who never could finish what he started, talked and wrote and explained, on and on, of what might have been if—if—if. Hooker strutted about like some injured Napoleon, blaming his subordinates for his failures. Longstreet, who sulkily had dragged his feet at Gettysburg and partly redeemed himself at Chickamauga, grumbled and complained to the bitter end. Grant went on to the White House, suffering a harrowing period of money troubles, thence to an echoing, domed tomb in New York. Hood passed to his reward with haunting ghosts in his sorrowful eyes. Each and all had trod their brief moment on the stage of life; each and all returned to the dust that triumphs over bugs and emperors alike.

William Sherman and Joseph Johnston, though the hardiest of mortal foes in battle, were the warmest friends in personal life.

In a brownstone mansion in New York City, Sherman lay dying of asthma. It was February 14, 1891, St. Valentine's Day. In less than a week he would have reached his seventy-first birthday. At 1:30 P.M. he insisted on getting out of bed and sitting in his favorite easy chair. At 1:50 he was dead.

His funeral was delayed five days pending the arrival of Sherman's son, Tom. After the Roman Catholic ritual, the black, silver-handled coffin was borne outside into the cold, windy day. Just outside the entrance foyer, hat in hand, stood the tall, spare figure of Joseph E. Johnston, one of the honorary pallbearers. His hair was snow-white now, his trim goatee scant and frosty.

A Union brigadier general laid his hand gently on Johnston's arm. "General," the Yankee officer urged, "please put on your hat—you'll get sick in this weather."

At that moment, Sherman's coffin was passing by. It paused a second beside Johnston. The old Confederate warrior, his eyes misty, nodded toward it. "If I were in there," he told the Union brigadier, "and he were standing here, he'd have his hat off."

Five weeks later Joe Johnston was dead—of pneumonia.

Index

Acworth, Ga.—20
Adairsville, Ga.—18
Adams, Gen.—84
Adamsville, Ga.—67
Alabama—2, 10, 39
Alabama (raider)—11
Alabama St.—67
Allatoona—18, 20, 23, 78, 83, 84
Anderson Ave.—66, 67
Andersonville—3, 80
Arkansas—2, 34
Army of the Cumberland (Union)
—12, 15, 29, 32, 33, 43, 56, 60, 72
Army of the Ohio (Union)—12, 41, 43, 56
Army of the Tennessee (Union)—12, 16, 43, 53, 56, 59, 66, 72
Ashby St.—51
Atlanta—4, 9-11, 13, 25, 29, 39, 43, 51, 52, 57, 58, 68, 69, 71, 72, 78. *Also* 1-91 *passim.*
Atlanta & West Point R.R.—10, 72, 73, 81
Atlanta Ave.—51, 53
Atlanta Home Guard—1, 11, 38
Atlanta Medical College—67
Atlanta Police Academy—57
Atlantic Coast Line R.R.—67
Auburn Ave.—69
Augusta, Ga.—7, 10, 47

Baltimore, Md.—59, 60
Bankhead Highway—39

Bate, Gen. Wm. B.—49, 58, 59, 72
Beaureguard, Gen. P. G. T.—84
Big Shanty, Ga.—20, 83
Blair, Gen. Frank P.—50, 58, 59
Blue Ridge Mountains—6
Bolton, Ga.—41
Boston, Mass.—9
Bouldercrest Dr., Rd.—57, 58
Boulevard Dr.—51, 75
Bragg, Maj. Gen. Braxton—6, 11, 38, 43, 46
Briarcliff Rd.—49, 53, 59
Brighton Rd.—48-50
Broad St.—27
Bryant County—89
Buck Head Creek—89
Buckhead (Atlanta)—43, 47, 48

Calhoun, Mayor James M.—75
Campbellton, Ga.—41
Candler Bldg.—69
Candler Park—58
Capitol Ave.—57
Car Shed—69
Carter, Gen.—84
Cartersville, Ga.—18
Cascade Rd.—72
Cassville, Ga.—18
Chapel Rd.—66
Charleston, S. C.—10, 47
Chattahoochee River—35, 39, 41, 43, 48, 72, 75
Chattanooga, Tenn.—2, 3, 6, 7, 10, 15, 25, 37, 68, 71, 83

92

Cheatham, Maj. Gen. B. F.—33, 34, 53, 57, 62, 67
Chickamauga, Ga.—2, 7, 38, 46, 47, 84, 90
City Hall (Atlanta)—78
City Point, Va.—2, 4
Clay St.—58
Clear Creek—48, 49
Cleburne Ave.—59
Cleburne, Gen. Pat—29, 31, 33, 49, 56-60, 62, 73, 84, 90
Clinton, Ga.—89
Cobb, Maj. Gen. Howell—80
Cogswell, Col. Wm.—78
Collier Rd.—48, 49
Columbia, Ala.—84
Columbus, Ga.—15
Coosa River—84
Covington, Ga.—87
Crawford W. Long Hospital—69
Crest Lawn Cemetery—48
Cross Keys Rd.—47
Crossroads Baptist Church—47
Cumberland Cavalry Corps (Union) —12
Custer, George—90
Cypress Swamp—89

Dallas, Ga.—20
Dalton, Ga.—10-12, 15, 16, 25, 27, 37, 46, 84
D'Alvigney, Dr. Noel—67
Davis, Jefferson—38, 46, 47, 49, 81, 83
Davisboro, Ga.—89
Decatur, Ga.—43, 47, 49, 53, 56-58, 62
Decatur St.—75, 85
DeGress Ave.—62
DeKalb Ave.—53, 60, 62
Dodge, Gen.—53, 58

East Atlanta—57, 58
East Atlanta Primitive Baptist Church—62
East Point, Ga.—66, 72, 73
Eden, Ga.—89

Eighth St.—69
Elliott St.—69
Ellis St.—39, 67
Etowah River—18, 26
Ezra Church—66-68, 72

Fayetteville Rd.—53, 57, 58, 62
Federal Prison (Atlanta)—57
Fifteenth Corps (Union)—12, 47, 53, 60, 62, 66, 67, 72
Five Points (Atlanta)—9, 52, 57, 67
Flat Shoals Ave.—48, 53, 57, 59
Flint River—73
Florence, Ala.—84
Forrest, Maj. Gen. Nathan B.—38
Forsyth, Ga.—65
Forsyth St.—69
Fort Beaulieu—89
Fort McAllister—89
Fort McPherson—60
Fort Rosedew—89
Fourteenth Corps (Union)—12, 48
Fourth Corps (Union)—12, 15, 48
Franklin, Tenn.—84
Fulton Bag & Cotton Mills—75

Gadsden, Ala.—84
Garrard, Brig. Gen. Kenner—41
Georgia Militia—1, 38, 39, 57, 73
Georgia R.R.—10, 47, 48, 51, 53, 60, 62
Gettysburg, Pa.—6, 84, 90
Gist, Gen.—84
Glenwood Ave.—48, 58
Gordon, Gen. John B.—1
Gordon Rd.—67
Granbury, Gen.—84
Grant Bldg.—27
Grant, Col. Lemuel P.—52
Grant Park—52, 62
Grant, Lt. Gen. Ulysses S.—2, 4, 6, 7, 10, 47, 87, 90
Green's Ferry Rd.—39, 66
Gresham, Brig. Gen. Walter Q.—56
Griffin, Ga.—15
Griswoldville, Ga.—89

Halleck, Gen.—87

Hardee, Lt. Gen. Wm. J.—13, 18, 27, 49, 56-58, 62, 73, 89, 90

Harker, Brig. Gen. Charles G.—33

Harrison, Col. Benjamin—49

Highland Ave.—48

Hinesville, Ga.—89

Hood, Lt. Gen. John B.—7, 13, 27, 29, 46-50, 56, 62, 64-68, 71-73, 79-81, 83, 84, 90

Hooker, Gen. Joe—29, 32, 48, 60, 75, 90

Howard, Maj. Gen. Oliver O.—12, 48, 60, 84

Howell Mill Rd.—48, 49

Howell's Ferry Rd.—39, 66

Hubner, Maj. Charles W.—46

Hurt, George M. Troup—62

Ida (steamer)—89

Indiana—3, 4, 41

Iowa Sixteenth Regiment (Union) —59

Iverson, Gen. Alfred—81

Ivy St.—39, 67

Jackson, Gen. Stonewall—60, 90

Jackson, Brig. Gen. W. H.—13, 43, 66, 80

Johnson's Ferry—41

Johnston, Gen. Joseph E.—1, 7, 9-13, 15, 16, 18, 20, 22, 23, 25-27, 31, 34, 35, 37-39, 41, 43, 46-48, 72, 80, 81, 91

Jonesboro, Ga.—65, 72, 73, 80, 89

Kennesaw, Ga.—22

Kennesaw Mtn.—23, 25-29, 31-34, 37, 39, 48, 51, 65

Kentucky—2, 3

Key Rd.—57

Kingston, Ga.—18, 84

Knoxville, Tenn.—15

Lay's Ferry—16

Lee, Gen. Robert E.—1, 3, 4, 6, 9-11, 47, 90

Lee, Lt. Gen. Stephen D.—66-68, 73

Leggett, Brig. Gen. Mortimer—59

Leggett's Hill—53, 56, 58, 59, 62

Lickskillet Rd.—67

Lincoln, Abraham—25

Logan, Maj. Gen. John A.—12, 53, 60, 62

Longstreet, Gen. James—6, 46, 47, 90

Lookout Mtn., Tenn.—2

Loring, Maj. Gen. W. W.—13, 49

Lost Mtn.—22, 27

Louisiana—2, 3, 27

Louisville Courier-Journal—15

Louisville, Ga.—89

Lovejoy's Station, Ga.—65, 73, 75, 78, 81

Luckie, Solomon—67

Macon, Ga.—10, 15, 65, 80, 81, 89

Macon & Western R.R.—10, 73, 80

Madison, Ga.—89

Manassas, Va.—6

Maney, Brig. Gen. George—49, 58, 59

Marietta, Ga.—18, 26, 41, 78, 83

Marietta National Cemetery—33

Marietta St.—43, 69, 75, 78

Martin Luther King, Jr. Dr.—66

Martin, Thomas H.—71

Martin, Col. W. H.—34

Mayson-Turner Ferry—39, 41

McClellan, George B.—90

McCook, Col. Daniel—33

McCook, Maj. Gen. Edward M.—80, 81

McDonough Rd.—57, 73

McPherson Ave.—60

McPherson, Maj. Gen. James B.—12, 15, 16, 29, 32, 41, 43, 47, 49, 53, 56, 58-60, 64, 66, 85, 90

Memorial Dr.—57, 58

Memphis, Tenn.—15, 37

Mercer, Maj. Gen. Hugh—58, 59
Milledgeville, Ga.—65, 89
Millen, Ga.—89
Mississippi—2, 39
Mitchell St.—78
Mobile, Ala.—6, 10
Monteith Swamp—89
Montgomery Ferry Rd.—39
Monument Ave.—60
Moore, J. C.—43
Moore's Mill Rd.—48
Moreland Ave.—48, 53, 56-58, 60, 62, 73
Morgan, John Hunt—2
Mosby, John S.—2
Mount Vernon Highway—47
Mozley Dr.—66
Mozley Park—66, 67

Nancy's Creek—43, 47
Nashville, Tenn.—16, 25, 37, 41, 46, 84
New Hope Church—20, 23, 37, 83
New Orleans, La.—6
New York City—4, 9, 90, 91
Newnan, Ga.—80
Nickajack Creek—39
Noonday Creek—29
Norfleet Rd.—49
Norfolk, Va.—10
North Ave. (Atlanta)—58, 66
North Ave. (East Point)—66
North Decatur Rd.—49, 59
North Highland Ave.—48, 59
Northside Dr.—48, 49

Oakland Cemetery—52
Ogeechee—89
Ohio Cavalry Div. (Union)—12, 41
Oostanaula River—16

Paces Ferry—43, 48
Palmer, Maj. Gen. John M.—48
Palmetto, Ga.—81
Paulding County—18
Peachtree Creek—39, 47, 48, 50, 53, 56

Peachtree Golf Club—47
Peachtree Rd.—47-50
Peachtree St.—57, 67, 69, 75
Pennsylvania—6, 31
Piedmont Hospital—50
Piedmont Park—49
Pilgrim, I. B.—71
Pine Mountain—22, 27
Plaza Park—69
Polk, Gen. Leonidas—13, 27, 29, 49
Ponce de Leon Ave.—51, 58
Pooler, Ga.—89
Powers Ferry—41, 43, 47
Pryor St.—69

Reed, Wallace P.—68, 69
Resaca, Ga.—15, 16, 37, 84
Resolute (steamer)—89
Rhodes St.—69
Richmond, Va.—9, 38, 43, 81
Ringgold, Ga.—3, 11, 12, 15
Rocky Face, Ga.—15
Rosecrans, Maj. Gen. Wm. S.—7
Roswell, Ga.—4, 41, 47
Rough and Ready, Ga.—72, 78

Sadie G. Mays Memorial Nursing Home—66-68
St. Luke's Episcopal Church—27
Sandersville, Ga.—89
Sandtown (Atlanta)—41, 72
Savannah, Ga.—10, 79, 87, 89, 90
Schofield, Maj. Gen. John M.—12, 41, 43, 47, 71, 72
Scott, Gen.—6
Selma, Ala.—15
Seventeenth Corps (Union)—12, 47, 53, 56, 66
Sherman, Maj. Gen. Wm. T.—2, 4, 7, 18, 20, 27, 35, 41, 47, 59, 68, 75, 85, 87, 91. Also 1-91 passim.
Shoup, Brig. Gen. F. A.—13
Sixteenth Corps (Union)—12, 47, 53, 60, 66
Slocum, Maj. Gen. Henry W.—75, 84

Smith, Brig. Gen. Giles A.—56, 59, 60-62
Smith, Maj. Gen. Gustavus W.—73
Smyrna, Ga.—39
Snake Creek Gap—15, 16
Sope Creek—41
South Carolina—80, 90
South River—57
Spring Hill, Tenn.—84
Spring St.—48, 57
Springfield, Ga.—89
Statesboro, Ga.—89
Stevens, Maj. Gen. C. H.—49
Stewart, Gen. A. P. —49, 67, 68, 73
Stone Mountain, Ga.—47, 49
Stoneman, Maj. Gen. George—12, 26, 41, 80, 81
Strahl, Gen.—84
Stuart, J. E. B.—2, 90
Sweeney, Brig. Gen. Thomas W.— 58, 59

Tanyard Branch—48, 49
Tennessee—2, 3, 39, 83
Tenth St.—58
Terry's Mill Pond—58
Thomas, Maj. Gen. Geo. H.—12, 15, 29, 32, 43, 47, 49, 58, 71, 75
Tupelo, Miss.—6, 84
Twenty-third Corps (Union)—12, 41, 53, 60
Twentieth Corps (Union)—12, 48, 83

Vernon River—89
Vicksburg, Miss.—52
Virginia—2-4, 6, 7, 9, 10, 12, 25, 47

Walker High School—57
Walker, Maj. Gen. W. H. T.—49, 58, 59, 64
Wall St.—69
Walthall, Maj. Gen. Ed. C.—49
Walton St.—27
Warren, Mr.—69
Washington, D. C.—2, 9, 35, 87
Washington St.—29, 78
Watterson, Henry—15
Waynesboro, Ga.—89
Weldon, N. C.—6
West Lake Ave.—66
West Point, Ga.—65
Western & Atlantic R.R.—10, 16, 20, 25, 26, 37-39, 43, 48, 51, 79, 81, 83, 85
Westview Cemetery—67
Wheat St.—69
Wheeler, Lt. Gen. Joseph—13, 26, 41, 43, 53, 56-58, 62, 72, 80, 89
White House, the—90
Whitefoord Ave.—53
Wilkinson Dr.—58
Williams, Brig. Gen. Alpheus S.—60
Williams Mill Rd.—49
Wilmington, N. C.—10, 47

Zimmer Dr.—48